Social and Emotional Learning Lesson Student Packet

Upper Grades (educator's discretion)

Educators need access to the internet and a screen and projector with sound for the lessons.

Print the packets out for distribution to students, and the rest of the work is done!

Created by: Melissa Marini Švigelj-Smith
2017-2019

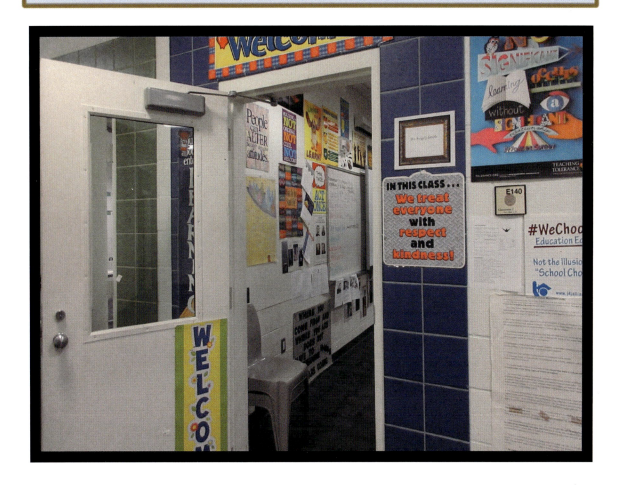

Life itself is your teacher, and you are in a state of constant learning.
~Bruce Lee

Copyright March 6, 2019 TX 8-714-430
Case # 1-7477515561

50 Social and Emotional Learning Mini Lesson Student Packets for Upper Grade Levels

Advisory and Social and Emotional Learning Curriculum for an Empowering Education

Melissa Marini Švigelj-Smith

Introduction to Social and Emotional Learning/Advisory Student Packets

A lot changed during the two decades I taught in high schools throughout Cleveland Public Schools, but one thing remained consistent: kids do better when they believe their teachers care and are interested in them as human beings. It seemed easier before our era of high-stakes standardized testing to make time for those important human connections in classrooms. As we begin to circle back to the importance of social and emotional learning, schools are being more purposeful about making time for relationship-building in classrooms. As an educator for four years in our county's juvenile detention center, social and emotional learning and practices were a necessary and crucial component for positive academic experiences in our classroom.

At convenings around the country, I present and discuss the trauma-informed and social and emotional learning approach I adopted in my classroom. After some of these gatherings, questions from attendees prompted me to contemplate how I could offer practical tools for teachers already overwhelmed and overworked by the demands of the profession. I know how many 12 hour days I worked during the school year, and integrating social and emotional learning should not add to those hours. What if there was an advisory resource book of student packets, with a variety of topics to choose from, for teachers to copy and have ready for students? These handouts attempt to fill that gap. The subjects may or may not fit exactly into traditional content areas, but they will offer perspectives around a variety of themes that often interest students. I was fortunate enough to have time built into my class schedule to focus on social and emotional learning competencies. When I reviewed students' schedules from the schools in their communities, I also saw courses such as "advisory," daily living," "life skills," and "employability." Although I adore having the creative freedom to develop a course of that nature, not all educators have that same inclination or the time to make it happen.

My hope and intent is that these student packets can be used as a resource when developing curriculum around social and emotional competencies, or at the very least, reduce the workloads of the educators who are designated to teach them.

My approach to teaching has been profoundly influenced by Brazilian educator, Paulo Freire. Freire's ideas of democratic or empowering education have been a catalyst for these packets, which were always meant to instigate and allow for discussion in my classroom. We often paused videos and the news to listen to each other's thoughts and questions. Freire's central premise is that education is not neutral and takes place in the context of people's lives. Wallerstein and Bernstein (1988) best summarize this philosophy:

> Freire asks, who does education serve and for what purpose? Does education socialize people to be objects and accept their limited roles within the status quo, or does it encourage people to question critical issues of the day and fully participate in the social and political life of society? To Freire, the purpose of education should be human liberation so that learners can be subjects and actors in their own lives and in society. To promote this role, Freire proposes a dialogue approach in which everyone participates as equals and colearners to create social knowledge. The goal of group dialogue is critical thinking by posing problems in such a way as to have participants uncover root causes of their place in society-the socioeconomic, political, cultural, and historical context of personal lives. But critical thinking continues beyond perception -towards the

actions that people take to move beyond powerlessness and gain control over their lives (pgs. 381-382).

The next few pages offer some explanations and research to support the daily packet templates included. It is also important to note that I taught young men ages 16-21 at our county's juvenile detention center for four years, so some of the content and language in the videos that correspond with the handouts may be more appropriate for older and less conservative students. Educators and other users of the handouts should **always** preview the content of the videos before using them with students.

It is equally important for me to mention that I do not purport or pretend to have a magic formula that will instantly make students adept at social and emotional competencies. Everyone should teach and interact with youth in accordance with their own zones of comfort and personality. All I am offering are resources that have worked for me, and the hope they will be useful for someone else.

From the Collaborative for Academic, Social, and Emotional Learning (CASEL) (2017):

- **Self - Awareness** - The ability to accurately recognize one's own emotions, thoughts, and values and how they influence behavior. The ability to accurately assess one's strengths and limitations, with a well-grounded sense of confidence, optimism, and a "growth mindset."
- **Self - Management** - The ability to successfully regulate one's emotions, thoughts, and behaviors in different situations — effectively managing stress, controlling impulses, and motivating oneself. The ability to set and work toward personal and academic goals.
- **Social Awareness** - The ability to take the perspective of and empathize with others, including those from diverse backgrounds and cultures. The ability to understand social and ethical norms for behavior and to recognize family, school, and community resources and supports.
- **Relationship Skills** - The ability to establish and maintain healthy and rewarding relationships with diverse individuals and groups. The ability to communicate clearly, listen well, cooperate with others, resist inappropriate social pressure, negotiate conflict constructively, and seek and offer help when needed.

- **Responsible Decision Making** - The ability to make constructive choices about personal behavior and social interactions based on ethical standards, safety concerns, and social norms. The realistic evaluation of consequences of various actions, and a consideration of the well-being of oneself and others.

*From http://www.casel.org/core-competencies/

Every day in my class we started with a daily gratitude statement. Why is gratitude important for students? Beginning each day with this small and quick activity was my attempt to mitigate negative energy, and to have students start from a positive place. According to the Harvard Health Journal, "*With gratitude, people acknowledge the goodness in their lives. In the process, people usually recognize that the source of that goodness lies at least partially outside themselves. As a result, gratitude also helps people connect to something larger than themselves as individuals — whether to other people, nature, or a higher power.*" My intention with students was to create habits during their adolescent years connected to gratitude, so that as students moved into more emotionally mature years they could cultivate a perspective associated with people who are grateful. According to Psychology Today, "Fostering gratitude can also broaden your thinking, and create positive cycles of thinking and behaving in healthy, positive ways." In education spaces, and in a world often fraught with negative images flashing across screens, more gratitude in our attitudes could improve everyone's health and happiness.

As the director of the Arizona Center for Integrative Medicine at the University of Arizona, the Harvard educated Dr. Andrew Weil is an internationally recognized expert on how to live a healthy life. Upon arrival to class, I taught students his 4-7-8 breathing exercise, which acts as a natural tranquilizer for the nervous system. I also reminded students every day on their papers to practice the 4-7-8 breathing method by including a brief summary of the exercise. Throughout the school year, we revisited the breathing exercise and its benefits through video examples. Students who arrived to me at the detention center were in varying states of trauma and their anxiety levels often fluctuated. Giving them a simple and natural tool to calm themselves, that may have even helped with sleeping, was a crucial component of a trauma-informed classroom, and is also a useful life skill for all of us. Here is how Dr. Weil describes the 4-7-8 breathing exercise:

- Exhale completely through your mouth, making a whoosh sound.
- Close your mouth and inhale quietly through your nose to a mental count of **four**.
- Hold your breath for a count of **seven**.
- Exhale completely through your mouth, making a whoosh sound to a count of **eight**. This is one breath.
- Now inhale again and repeat the cycle three more times for a total of four breaths.

As a Stanford University psychologist, Carol Dweck is widely renowned for her research into human motivation and what she termed *growth mindset*. Teaching students they are not born with a fixed level of intelligence, and that we are all born to learn and develop our abilities was enlightening for many of my students. At the detention center, there were times when 75% of the students in my classroom had been labeled with various special education designations. Offering them the knowledge that ANYONE can get better, regardless of what they had been labeled or told previously, nourished the possibility for positive academic experiences and made accomplishment seem less elusive. I still correspond with former students who mention *growth mindset* as a concept that drives them. Thus, we started off the school year with studying *growth mindset*, and their packets had a simple reminder everyday of what it means to have a *growth mindset* versus a *fixed mindset.* As new students arrived, I reviewed the concept with them and we had large group lessons focused on growth mindset throughout the school year to refresh our memories about the power of mindset.

Particularly for youth pushed out of schools, a trend of low self esteem related to academics manifested in my classroom. It is important to mention that teaching about growth mindset without implementing additional actions to begin to rebuild the academic confidence that has been deteriorating, or has been decimated, over the course of students' school years may be too narrow of an approach to yield results. Society wrongly reinforces messages that assault the intellectual abilities of some demographics, and schools are generally arranged to reproduce inequities. It takes a tremendous amount of diligence to begin to overcome harmful labels which have been reducing the confidence of students for years. Students must be celebrated and feel safe and worthy of celebration. They must know and feel that they matter. Thus, our daily videos were often reflective of their experiences and representative of their backgrounds, yet relevant and informative to everyone watching. Links to the free videos and the length of time for the videos are available in each student packet. Answer keys are not included because all videos should be previewed before being shown to students. I encourage educators to watch the videos and create answer keys to be used if needed or desired.

The CNN news show, *CNN 10,* was included in our daily class routine because it was important to me that students remain aware of the world outside of the concrete walls we existed within during the school day, and during their time at the detention center. The show is described as a global news show for a global audience of students and is free to watch each school day on http://www.cnn.com/cnn10. It is updated each school day, presents unbiased news stories, and is sensitive to a young viewing audience. Although students sometimes complained about the host's "corny" puns, several students also continued to indicate that the news was one of their favorite parts of the school day. Particularly for some students, exposure to a larger world may have played a role in their development as individuals or their future aspirations. Writing five things they learned from the ten-minute news show kept them focused and guided them to practice their listening and writing skills.

When students arrived to my class, I asked them to complete a student-interest survey in order to gain information about what intrigued them, their feelings towards school, and goals for their future. I never had a student write that they wanted to quit school or did not want to learn. So why do some students persist and others seem to fade away? Of course, knowing an adult believes in them and cares makes a difference, but that is not enough. Students wrote on their interest surveys that they wanted to be doctors, lawyers, veterinarians, and entrepreneurs. Yet, many were not able to formulate the actionable steps necessary to accomplish their goals after high school. Thus, I created a daily goals chart for students to complete as part of their daily activities. I intentionally placed the goals section of the student packets after sections they would have completed, so that everyone had a chance to "check-off" accomplishments. Students checked (✔) that they had written their daily gratitude, completed their video questions, and wrote CNN student news facts. We moved on to a literacy activity after they wrote their own personal goals.

The daily goal exercise (which includes daily "I Can" statements) is simple, but it serves not only as an avenue for students to experience success, it also provides an opportunity for them to see how focusing on specific tasks each day can assist them with reaching their future goals. Writing the words down also assisted students with visualizing helpful choices and actions during the school day. Dividing the goals into an academic and behavior section illustrated for students the connection between their attitudes and accomplishing goals while also providing multiple opportunities to achieve. A student's behavior goal might have been to not get distracted by others, and their academic goal might have been to earn an "A" on a test in math, so even if they earned a "C" on their math test, they still had an opportunity to declare success in their reflection writings.

The final portion of our daily routine included a student self-reflection. The self-reflection begins with a way for students to have a daily reminder that they did something well. Students are asked to rate themselves and to explain why. Rarely were there instances in which students were not completely honest. Often, I found that students were harder on themselves than I would have been. In alignment with practicing a "growth mindset," students are also asked to write about something they would like to improve. This reminds them we all have room to grow, and learning from our mistakes is part of life; not a deficiency. Finally, students had an opportunity to share something with me by completing one of the sentence starters. The design leaves room for a range of responses from celebratory to personal. Many student responses further informed my instructional strategies and approaches. These reflections should also be completed in a relationship of trust. Their responses are for their teacher - not a future book their teacher wants to publish. Jails for children, schools for survival, and the prison industrial complex should be abolished. Until that happens, the least we can do as educators is plant hope and grow love in a garden of trust.

Works Cited

2017, Casel. "Core SEL Competencies." *Casel*, 1 Jan. 2017, www.casel.org/core-competencies/.

Dweck, Carol S.. *Mindset: The New Psychology Of Success*. New York : Ballantine Books, 2008. Print.

Greenberg, Melanie. "How Gratitude Leads to a Happier Life." *Psychology Today*, Sussex Publishers, 22 Nov. 2015, www.psychologytoday.com/blog/the-mindful-self-express/201511/how-gratitude-leads-happier-life.

Simon, Harvey B. "Giving Thanks Can Make You Happier." *Harvard Health*, Harvard Health Publishing, 1 Nov. 2017, www.health.harvard.edu/healthbeat/giving-thanks-can-make-you-happier.

Wallerstein, N., & Bernstein, E. (1988). Empowerment Education: Freire's Ideas Adapted to Health Education. Health Education Quarterly, 15(4), 379–394. https://doi.org/10.1177/109019818801500402

Weil, Andrew. "Breathing Exercise: Three To Try | 4-7-8 Breath | Andrew Weil, M.D."*DrWeil.com*, WEIL, 3 Nov. 2017, www.drweil.com/health-wellness/body-mind-spirit/stress-anxiety/breathing-three-exercises/.

CONTENTS

Pages 1-7: Introduction to the lessons and works cited

Mini Lesson Topics 1-50

Each lesson has a video and focus questions for students to answer.

1. A Difference From an Unusual Place - Luis Gonzalez TED Talk (9 minutes)
2. A Good Role Model of What Not to Do | Wilfredo Laracuente | TEDxSingSing (7 minutes)
3. Adam Foss: A prosecutor's vision for a better justice system TED Talk (16 minutes)
4. After watching this, your brain will not be the same | Lara Boyd (14 minutes)
5. All it Takes is 10 Mindful Minutes: Andy Puddicombe TED Talk (9 minutes)
6. Brain Games - Season 2 Episode 6 What you don't know (21 minutes)
7. Brain Games Season 2 Episode 1 Focus Pocus (22 minutes)
8. Belly Breathe with Common and Colbie Callait (2 mins)

    4 Steps to Developing a Growth Mindset? (4 mins)

    Am I Not Human? A call for criminal justice reform, Marlon Peterson TEDxTalk (7.5 mins)
9. Bruce Talks Candidly About His Time in Prison and Life on the Streets | Released | OWN (4.5 minutes)
10. Bryan Stevenson: We Need to Talk About an Injustice TED Talk (24 minutes)
11. Carry On - An ESPN short film in Cleveland, Ohio (21 minutes)
12. Chess & Community: the power of a single hour/Lemuel LaRoche TEDTalk (16 minutes)
13. Clint Smith: The Danger of Silence TED Talk (4 minutes)
14. Dan Gross: Why Gun Violence Can't Be Our New Normal (13:39 mins)
15. Dan Phillips: Creative houses from reclaimed stuff (18 minutes)
16. Dare to Dream Again, Prophet Walker TED Talk (6 minutes)
17. David Gallo: Underwater astonishments (5 minutes) TED Talk
18. Epigenetics and the Influence of Our Genes - Courtney Griffins TEDx (18 minutes)
19. ESPN E60 - Four Weeks in Ferguson (11 minutes)
20. ESPN 30 for 30 -Ghosts of 'Ole Miss (50 minutes)
21. ESPN E60 - Love is Stronger, Chris Singleton (30 mins)
22. Facing Fear - Sean Wilson (5 mins)
23. 4 Thoughts About Gratitude That Could Change Your Life | Digital Original | Oprah Winfrey Network (2.5 minutes)

    Breathing Space: Solitude on the Pacific Crest Trail | SuperSoul Sunday | Oprah Winfrey

Created by **Melissa Marini Švigelj-Smith** 2017-2019

Network (1.5 minutes)

24. Fox Sports Tour of Negro League Baseball Museum (6 minutes)
25. Freeman Hrabowski: 4 pillars of college success in science (& in school) (15 minute TED Talk)
26. Friends (spoken word) by Suli Breaks (3 minutes)
27. Grateful for the Opportunity, M. Clark (5 minutes)
28. Heroes & Villains: Is Hip Hop a Cancer or a Cure? Lecrae (18 minute TED Talk)
29. Hip Hop & Shakespeare? Akala at TEDxAldeburgh (20 minutes)
30. How I Help Free Innocent People from Prison: Ronald Sullivan (12 minutes) TEDx Talk
31. Human Stories Behind Mass Incarceration, TED Talk (13:39 mins)
32. Edith Widder: How we found the giant squid (9 minutes) TED Talk
    David Gallo: Underwater astonishments (5 minutes) TED Talk (also a single lesson #16)
33. It's Your Turn to Listen? Deonta Bell (9 minutes)
34. Joe Ehrmann: Be A Man (14 minutes)
35. John Legend - Redemption Song TED Talk (9 minutes)
36. Jose Miguel Sokoloff: How Christmas Lights Helped Guerrillas Put Down Their Guns (14 minute TED Talk)
37. Josh Luber: The secret sneaker market — and why it matters (12 minute TED Talk)
38. Laurel Braitman - TED Talk (20 minutes)
    Depressed Dogs, Cats with OCD - What we can learn about humans from animals
39. Life Lessons from an Incarcerated Father: Last Chance High Episode 6 (12 minutes)
40. Lift Off, Donovan Livingston at his Harvard graduation, Poem (4 minutes)
41. Marshall Davis Jones: Spelling Father, Poem on Vimeo (3.5 mins)
42. Nature. Beauty. Gratitude. TED Talk (8 minutes)
43. Native Prisoners of War in America: Aaron Huey TED Talk (15 minutes)
44. The Nightmare Videos of Children's YouTube, TED Talk (14 mins)
45. Unflinching Look at Racial Violence from an Artist - TED Talk (4 minutes)
46. What a World without Prisons Could Look Like - TED Talk (15 mins)
47. What I learned as a kid in jail: Ismael Nazario TED Talk (11 mins)
48. What if we ended the injustice of bail? (14 mins)
49. What really matters at the end of life? - TED Talk (19 mins)
50. Writing my wrongs - Shaka Senghor TEDxMidwest (18 minutes)
    ***BONUS - The Science of Happiness (8 minutes)

Name_____ Date_____

Write one thing you are grateful (**thankful**) for today. Finding things to be thankful for helps improve our overall happiness. Happier people are more successful people._____
_____

Today I am thankful for role models.

Remember to practice 4-7-8 breathing as needed, and to keep a growth mindset.

> **Develop a GROWTH MINDSET -** *People who believe their talents can be developed (through hard work, good strategies & input from others) have a growth mindset. They tend to achieve more than those with a fixed mindset. ~Dr. Carol Dweck*

Instead of thinking...	Try thinking...
I give up	I won't stop until I succeed
I'm not good at this	How can I get better?
I can't be any better	I can always improve
This is too hard	This may take some time
I can't do this	I am going to learn to do this
My mistakes ruined me	I can learn from my mistakes
My plan didn't work	I can try another plan
I'm not smart	I can always learn new things
I'm jealous	I can learn from their success

[A Good Role Model of What Not to Do | Wilfredo Laracuente | TEDxSingSing](#)

(7 minutes)

1. How many children in America are being raised without a father?

2. What does Mr. Laracuente say we need to instill in our young people?

3. What did Mr. Laracuente say is needed in urban communities?

4. Which two types of people exist in everyone, according to Mr. Laracuente?

5. What kind of person are you striving to be?

Created by **Melissa Marini Švigelj-Smith** 2017-2019

CNN 10 STUDENT NEWS (10 minute show)
Write 5 things you learned from the news today.

1. _____
   _____
   _____
2. _____
   _____
   _____
3. _____
   _____
   _____
4. _____
   _____
   _____
5. _____
   _____
   _____

Daily Goals Sheet *I can statements for each day.
This is the list of things that I want to accomplish (complete) today in class.

Tasks or assignments I need to complete in class *I can exercise strategies like deep breathing (4-7-8 breathing) to calm or focus myself.	Completed? Check if "yes"
1. Entry journal prompt response & daily gratitude statement *I can recognize what I value and appreciate. *I can write a thoughtful & clear response to a writing prompt.	
2. Daily Goals Sheet filled out *I can plan short-term goals in order to reach my long term goals.	
3. CNN Student News Guided Notes 1-5 *I can summarize events in a news story.	
4. Close Reading/Literacy Activity: Today we are_____ _____ *I can complete a close reading or literacy strategy for something that I read. *I can organize and summarize information.	
Write your own goals for your school work for #s 5 and 6.	
5.	
6. *I can complete activities & lessons in my courses.	
7. Reflection sheet on goals today	

Created by **Melissa Marini Švigelj-Smith** 2017-2019

*I can reflect on my day and write honestly about whether or not I accomplished my short-term goals.	

In class today, my behavior goals are… Write your own personal goals for #s 3 & 4 *I can use strategies to maintain positive behaviors & reduce negative behaviors.	Did I …? Check if "yes"
1. I will keep a growth mindset.	
2. I will make healthy choices.	
3.	
4.	

DAILY REFLECTION

Explain what you did well today in at least one complete sentence. _____
_____

Explain how you would rate your performance in class today on a scale of 10 to 1, and explain why you ranked yourself that way. 10= I did my best 5= I tried half the time 1=I did not try at all
_____
_____

Write a complete sentence about one part of your work in class that you would like to improve and explain why.
_____
_____

Choose to complete at least ONE of the writing prompts below. Circle which one you are completing.
1. I wish that you would have known today that I…
2. I am really proud that today I…
3. My favorite part of today was…
4. I wonder if today I could...

_____
_____
_____

Created by **Melissa Marini Švigelj-Smith** 2017-2019

Name_____ Date_____

Write one thing you are grateful (**thankful**) for today. Finding things to be thankful for helps improve our overall happiness. Happier people are more successful people._____

_____

Today I'm thankful that I am here!

Remember to practice 4-7-8 breathing as needed, and to keep a growth mindset.

> **Develop a *GROWTH MINDSET*** - People who believe their talents can be developed (through hard work, good strategies & input from others) have a growth mindset. They tend to achieve more than those with a fixed mindset. ~Dr. Carol Dweck

Instead of thinking...	Try thinking...
I give up	I won't stop until I succeed
I'm not good at this	How can I get better?
I can't be any better	I can always improve
This is too hard	This may take some time
I can't do this	I am going to learn to do this
My mistakes ruined me	I can learn from my mistakes
My plan didn't work	I can try another plan
I'm not smart	I can always learn new things
I'm jealous	I can learn from their success

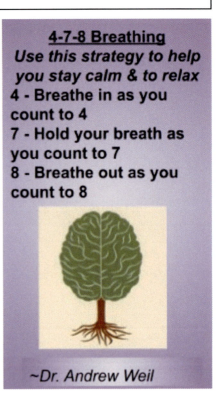

4-7-8 Breathing
Use this strategy to help you stay calm & to relax
4 - Breathe in as you count to 4
7 - Hold your breath as you count to 7
8 - Breathe out as you count to 8

~Dr. Andrew Weil

[A Difference From an Unusual Place - Luis Gonzalez](#) **TED Talk (9 minutes)**

1. At what age did Luis enter prison?

2. What did Luis want his mother to know?

3. How many scholarships have Luis and his colleagues awarded over 6 years?

4. Luis said that our country must invest in the education of _____ children.

5. Luis said that he is the true testament of the power of _____.

Created by Melissa Marini Švigelj-Smith 2017-2019

CNN 10 STUDENT NEWS (10 minute show)
Write 5 things you learned from the news today.

1. _____
   _____
2. _____
   _____
3. _____
   _____
4. _____
   _____
5. _____
   _____

Daily Goals Sheet   ***I can statements for each day.***

This is the list of things that I want to accomplish (complete) today in class.

Tasks or assignments I need to complete in class *I can exercise strategies like deep breathing (4-7-8 breathing) to calm or focus myself.	Completed? Check if "yes"
1. Entry journal prompt response & daily gratitude statement *I can recognize what I value and appreciate. *I can write a thoughtful & clear response to a writing prompt.	
2. Daily Goals Sheet filled out *I can plan short-term goals in order to reach my long term goals.	
3. CNN Student News Guided Notes 1-5 *I can summarize events in a news story.	
4. Close Reading/Literacy Activity: Today we are_____ _____ *I can complete a close reading or literacy strategy for something that I read. *I can organize and summarize information.	
Write your own goals for your school work for #s 5 and 6.	
5.	
6. *I can complete activities & lessons in my courses.	
7. Reflection sheet on goals today	

Created by **Melissa Marini Švigelj-Smith** 2017-2019

*I can reflect on my day and write honestly about whether or not I accomplished my short-term goals.	

In class today, my behavior goals are… Write your own personal goals for #s 3 & 4 *I can use strategies to maintain positive behaviors & reduce negative behaviors.	Did I …? Check if "yes"
1. I will keep a growth mindset.	
2. I will make healthy choices.	
3.	
4.	

DAILY REFLECTION

Explain what you did well today in at least one complete sentence. _____
_____

Explain how you would rate your performance in class today on a scale of 10 to 1, and explain why you ranked yourself that way. 10= I did my best 5= I tried half the time 1=I did not try at all
_____
_____

Write a complete sentence about one part of your work in class that you would like to improve and explain why.
_____
_____

Choose to complete at least ONE of the writing prompts below. Circle which one you are completing.
1. I wish that you would have known today that I…
2. I am really proud that today I…
3. My favorite part of today was…
4. I wonder if today I could...

_____
_____
_____

Name_____ Date_____

Write one thing you are grateful **(thankful)** for today. Finding things to be thankful for helps improve our overall happiness. Happier people are more successful people._____
_____

Today I am thankful for blue skies.
Remember to practice 4-7-8 breathing as needed, and to keep a growth mindset.

Develop a *GROWTH MINDSET* - *People who believe their talents can be developed (through hard work, good strategies & input from others) have a growth mindset. They tend to achieve more than those with a fixed mindset. ~Dr. Carol Dweck*

Instead of thinking...	Try thinking...
I give up	I won't stop until I succeed
I'm not good at this	How can I get better?
I can't be any better	I can always improve
This is too hard	This may take some time
I can't do this	I am going to learn to do this
My mistakes ruined me	I can learn from my mistakes
My plan didn't work	I can try another plan
I'm not smart	I can always learn new things
I'm jealous	I can learn from their success

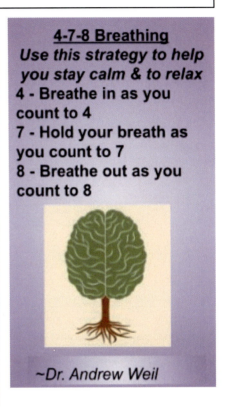

4-7-8 Breathing
Use this strategy to help you stay calm & to relax
4 - Breathe in as you count to 4
7 - Hold your breath as you count to 7
8 - Breathe out as you count to 8

~Dr. Andrew Weil

[Adam Foss: A prosecutor's vision for a better justice system](#) **TED Talk (16 minutes)**

1. What does Adam confess to?

2. 3. 4. Describe one thing that Adam says happened during his 1st, 2nd, and 3rd year of law school.

    A.

    B.

    C.

5. What was Adam's first case about?

6. What does Adam say most prosecutors never learn in their law classes?

7. Where was Christopher at 6 years later?

8. I learned the power of the prosecutor to _____ lives instead of ruining them.

Created by **Melissa Marini Švigelj-Smith** 2017-2019

9. 10. 11. According to Adam, what prosecutors do should matter to people because...

    A.

    B.

    C.

12. What type of prosecutor does Adam suggest to people that they should vote for?

CNN 10 STUDENT NEWS (10 minute show)
*Write **5** things you learned from the news today.*

1. _____

2. _____

3. _____

4. _____

5. _____

Daily Goals Sheet   *I can statements for each day.*
This is the list of things that I want to accomplish (complete) today in class.

Tasks or assignments I need to complete in class *I can exercise strategies like deep breathing (4-7-8 breathing) to calm or focus myself.	Completed? Check if "yes"
1. Entry journal prompt response & daily gratitude statement *I can recognize what I value and appreciate. *I can write a thoughtful & clear response to a writing prompt.	
2. Daily Goals Sheet filled out *I can plan short-term goals in order to reach my long term goals.	
3. CNN Student News Guided Notes 1-5 *I can summarize events in a news story.	
4. Close Reading/Literacy Activity: Today we are_____ *I can complete a close reading or literacy strategy for something that I read. *I can organize and summarize information.	
Write your own goals for your school work for #s 5 and 6.	

5.	
6. *I can complete activities & lessons in my courses.	
7. Reflection sheet on goals today *I can reflect on my day and write honestly about whether or not I accomplished my short-term goals.	

In class today, my behavior goals are… **Write your own personal goals for #s 3 & 4** *I can use strategies to maintain positive behaviors & reduce negative behaviors.	**Did I …? Check if "yes"**
1. I will keep a growth mindset.	
2. I will make healthy choices.	
3.	
4.	

DAILY REFLECTION

Explain what you did well today in at least one complete sentence. _____
_____

Explain how you would rate your performance in class today on a scale of 10 to 1, and explain why you ranked yourself that way. 10= I did my best 5= I tried half the time 1=I did not try at all
_____
_____

Write a complete sentence about one part of your work in class that you would like to improve and explain why.
_____
_____

Choose to complete at least ONE of the writing prompts below. Circle which one you are completing.
1. I wish that you would have known today that I…
2. I am really proud that today I…
3. My favorite part of today was…
4. I wonder if today I could...

_____
_____
_____

Created by **Melissa Marini Švigelj-Smith** 2017-2019

Name_____ Date_____

Write one thing you are grateful (**thankful**) for today. Finding things to be thankful for helps improve our overall happiness. Happier people are more successful people._____

_____

Today I am thankful for being able to make my brain work better.

Remember to practice 4-7-8 breathing as needed, and to keep a growth mindset.

> **Develop a *GROWTH MINDSET* - People who believe their talents can be developed (through hard work, good strategies & input from others) have a growth mindset. They tend to achieve more than those with a fixed mindset. ~Dr. Carol Dweck**

Instead of thinking...	Try thinking...
I give up	I won't stop until I succeed
I'm not good at this	How can I get better?
I can't be any better	I can always improve
This is too hard	This may take some time
I can't do this	I am going to learn to do this
My mistakes ruined me	I can learn from my mistakes
My plan didn't work	I can try another plan
I'm not smart	I can always learn new things
I'm jealous	I can learn from their success

After watching this, your brain will not be the same | Lara Boyd
(14 minutes)

1. True or false: when you're thinking of nothing, your brain is at rest.

    _____

2. And 3. What are TWO ways the brain can change?

4. What health event is it difficult for the brain to recover from?

5. What is the best driver of neuroplastic change in our brains?

6. Nothing is more effective than _____ in order to learn.

7. Behaviors that you employ in your everyday life are important because each of them is changing your _____.

8. Repeat behaviors that are _____ for your brain and break those habits that are not.

9. Everything you do and everything you encounter is _____ your brain for better or for worse. Build the brain you want!

CNN 10 STUDENT NEWS (10 minute show)
Write 5 things you learned from the news today.

1. _____
   _____
   _____

2. _____
   _____
   _____

3. _____
   _____
   _____

4. _____
   _____
   _____

5. _____
   _____
   _____

Daily Goals Sheet   *I can statements for each day.
This is the list of things that I want to accomplish (complete) today in class.

Tasks or assignments I need to complete in class *I can exercise strategies like deep breathing (4-7-8 breathing) to calm or focus myself.	Completed? Check if "yes"
1. Entry journal prompt response & daily gratitude statement *I can recognize what I value and appreciate. *I can write a thoughtful & clear response to a writing prompt.	
2. Daily Goals Sheet filled out *I can plan short-term goals in order to reach my long term goals.	
3. CNN Student News Guided Notes 1-5 *I can summarize events in a news story.	
4. Close Reading/Literacy Activity: Today we are_____ _____ *I can complete a close reading or literacy strategy for something that I read. *I can organize and summarize information.	
Write your own goals for your school work for #s 5 and 6.	

Created by **Melissa Marini Švigelj-Smith** 2017-2019

5.	
6. *I can complete activities & lessons in my courses.	
7. Reflection sheet on goals today *I can reflect on my day and write honestly about whether or not I accomplished my short-term goals.	

In class today, my behavior goals are… Write your own personal goals for #s 3 & 4 *I can use strategies to maintain positive behaviors & reduce negative behaviors.	**Did I …? Check if "yes"**
1. I will keep a growth mindset.	
2. I will make healthy choices.	
3.	
4.	

DAILY REFLECTION

Explain what you did well today in at least one complete sentence. _____
_____

Explain how you would rate your performance in class today on a scale of 10 to 1, and explain why you ranked yourself that way. 10= I did my best 5= I tried half the time 1=I did not try at all
_____
_____

Write a complete sentence about one part of your work in class that you would like to improve and explain why.
_____
_____

Choose to complete at least ONE of the writing prompts below. Circle which one you are completing.
1. I wish that you would have known today that I…
2. I am really proud that today I…
3. My favorite part of today was…
4. I wonder if today I could...

_____
_____
_____

Created by **Melissa Marini Švigelj-Smith** 2017-2019

Name_____Date_____

Write one thing you are grateful **(thankful)** for today. Finding things to be thankful for helps improve our overall happiness. Happier people are more successful people._____

_____

Today I am thankful for time to think.
Remember to practice 4-7-8 breathing as needed, and to keep a growth mindset.

Develop a *GROWTH MINDSET* - People who believe their talents can be developed (through hard work, good strategies & input from others) have a growth mindset. They tend to achieve more than those with a fixed mindset. ~Dr. Carol Dweck

Instead of thinking...	Try thinking...
I give up	I won't stop until I succeed
I'm not good at this	How can I get better?
I can't be any better	I can always improve
This is too hard	This may take some time
I can't do this	I am going to learn to do this
My mistakes ruined me	I can learn from my mistakes
My plan didn't work	I can try another plan
I'm not smart	I can always learn new things
I'm jealous	I can learn from their success

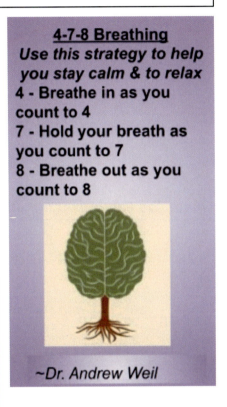

4-7-8 Breathing
Use this strategy to help you stay calm & to relax
4 - Breathe in as you count to 4
7 - Hold your breath as you count to 7
8 - Breathe out as you count to 8

~Dr. Andrew Weil

<u>All it Takes is 10 Mindful Minutes</u>: Andy Puddicombe TED Talk (9 minutes)

1. What do many of us not take enough time to look after?
2. How did Andy deal with the things in his life that were stressing him out when he was 20?
3. According to a Harvard study, how often are our minds lost in thought?
4. What is meditation?
5. What opportunity can meditation offer?

Created by **Melissa Marini Švigelj-Smith** 2017-2019

CNN 10 STUDENT NEWS (10 minute show)
Write 5 things you learned from the news today.

1. _____
   _____
   _____
2. _____
   _____
   _____
3. _____
   _____
   _____
4. _____
   _____
   _____
5. _____
   _____
   _____

Daily Goals Sheet   *****I can statements for each day.**

This is the list of things that I want to accomplish (complete) today in class.

Tasks or assignments I need to complete in class	Completed? Check if "yes"
*I can exercise strategies like deep breathing (4-7-8 breathing) to calm or focus myself.	
1. Entry journal prompt response & daily gratitude statement *I can recognize what I value and appreciate. *I can write a thoughtful & clear response to a writing prompt.	
2. Daily Goals Sheet filled out *I can plan short-term goals in order to reach my long term goals.	
3. CNN Student News Guided Notes 1-5 *I can summarize events in a news story.	
4. Close Reading/Literacy Activity: Today we are_____ _____ *I can complete a close reading or literacy strategy for something that I read. *I can organize and summarize information.	
Write your own goals for your school work for #s 5 and 6.	
5.	
6. *I can complete activities & lessons in my courses.	
7. Reflection sheet on goals today	

Created by **Melissa Marini Švigelj-Smith** 2017-2019

*I can reflect on my day and write honestly about whether or not I accomplished my short-term goals.	

In class today, my behavior goals are… **Write your own personal goals for #s 3 & 4** *I can use strategies to maintain positive behaviors & reduce negative behaviors.	**Did I …?** **Check if "yes"**
1. I will keep a growth mindset.	
2. I will make healthy choices.	
3.	
4.	

DAILY REFLECTION

Explain what you did well today in at least one complete sentence. _____
_____

Explain how you would rate your performance in class today on a scale of 10 to 1, and explain why you ranked yourself that way. 10= I did my best 5= I tried half the time 1=I did not try at all
_____
_____

Write a complete sentence about one part of your work in class that you would like to improve and explain why.
_____
_____

Choose to complete at least ONE of the writing prompts below. Circle which one you are completing.
1. I wish that you would have known today that I…
2. I am really proud that today I…
3. My favorite part of today was…
4. I wonder if today I could...

_____
_____
_____

Created by **Melissa Marini Švigelj-Smith** 2017-2019

Name_____Date_____

Write one thing you are grateful **(thankful)** for today. Finding things to be thankful for helps improve our overall happiness. Happier people are more successful people. _____
_____

Today I am thankful for the different colors that arrive with each season.

Develop a GROWTH MINDSET - *People who believe their talents can be developed (through hard work, good strategies & input from others) have a growth mindset. They tend to achieve more than those with a fixed mindset. ~Dr. Carol Dweck*

Instead of thinking...	Try thinking...
I give up	I won't stop until I succeed
I'm not good at this	How can I get better?
I can't be any better	I can always improve
This is too hard	This may take some time
I can't do this	I am going to learn to do this
My mistakes ruined me	I can learn from my mistakes
My plan didn't work	I can try another plan
I'm not smart	I can always learn new things
I'm jealous	I can learn from their success

Remember to practice 4-7-8 Breathing to assist with staying calm and focused and keep a growth mindset.

[Brain Games - Season 2 Episode 6 *What you don't know (21 minutes)*](#)

1. How did the kids know which direction the bus was going to go?

2. Why is the brain wired with an "illusion of knowledge"?

3. What is a mistake a student made when drawing a bike from memory?

4. What would your brain rather do than admit it doesn't know something?

5. How many books are in the Old Testament?

6. How many countries are in Africa?

7. What was wrong with the "NY" sign?

8. Why does your brain provide you the least amount of information necessary?

9. Which word was on the first and second train?

10. What was the point of this episode?

CNN 10 STUDENT NEWS (10 minute show)

Write 5 things you learned from the news today.

1. _____
   _____
   _____

2. _____
   _____
   _____

3. _____
   _____
   _____

4. _____
   _____
   _____

5. _____
   _____
   _____

Daily Goals Sheet   **I can statements for each day.*
This is the list of things that I want to accomplish (complete) today in class.

Tasks or assignments I need to complete in class	Completed? Check if "yes"
*I can exercise strategies like deep breathing (4-7-8 breathing) to calm or focus myself.	
1. Entry journal prompt response & daily gratitude statement *I can recognize what I value and appreciate. *I can write a thoughtful & clear response to a writing prompt.	
2. Daily Goals Sheet filled out *I can plan short-term goals in order to reach my long term goals.	
3. CNN Student News Guided Notes 1-5 *I can summarize events in a news story.	
4. Close Reading/Literacy Activity: Today we are_____ *I can complete a close reading or literacy strategy for something that I read. *I can organize and summarize information.	
Write your own goals for your school work for #s 5 and 6.	

5.	
6. *I can complete activities & lessons in my online courses.	
7. Reflection sheet on goals today *I can reflect on my day and write honestly about whether or not I accomplished my short-term goals.	

In class today, my behavior goals are… **Write your own personal goals for #s 3 & 4** *I can use strategies to maintain positive behaviors & reduce negative behaviors.	Did I …? Check if "yes"
1. I will keep a growth mindset.	
2. I will make healthy choices.	
3.	
4.	

DAILY REFLECTION

Explain what you did well today in at least one complete sentence. _____
_____

Explain how you would rate your performance in class today on a scale of 10 to 1, and explain why you ranked yourself that way. 10= I did my best 5= I tried half the time 1=I did not try at all
_____

Write a complete sentence about one part of your work in class that you would like to improve and explain why.
_____

Choose to complete ONE of the writing prompts below. Circle which one you are completing.
1. I wish that you would have known today that I…
2. I am really proud that today I…
3. My favorite part of today was…
4. I wonder if today I could...

_____
_____
_____

Name_____ Date_____

Write one thing you are grateful **(thankful)** for today. Finding things to be thankful for helps improve our overall happiness. Happier people are more successful people._____

_____

Today I am thankful for the brain's visual cortex.
Remember to practice 4-7-8 breathing as needed, and to keep a growth mindset.

> **Develop a *GROWTH MINDSET* -** *People who believe their talents can be developed (through hard work, good strategies & input from others) have a growth mindset. They tend to achieve more than those with a fixed mindset. ~Dr. Carol Dweck*

	Instead of thinking...		Try thinking...
	I give up		I won't stop until I succeed
	I'm not good at this		How can I get better?
	I can't be any better		I can always improve
	This is too hard		This may take some time
	I can't do this		I am going to learn to do this
	My mistakes ruined me		I can learn from my mistakes
	My plan didn't work		I can try another plan
	I'm not smart		I can always learn new things
	I'm jealous		I can learn from their success

Brain Games Season 2 Episode 1 *Focus Pocus* (22 minutes)

1. What is it called when you lose focus and attention?
2. What did *smooth pursuit* help our ancestors with?
3. How would the world look if the brain's visual cortex wasn't available?
4. What is 50% of the brain's visual cortex devoted to?
5. What is our peripheral vision weak at seeing?
6. What object is part of one of the most common continuity errors in scenes?
7. What does the narrator say you can do with what you've learned about the brain's focus?

CNN 10 STUDENT NEWS (10 minute show)
Write 5 things you learned from the news today.

1. _____
   _____
   _____
2. _____
   _____
   _____
3. _____
   _____
   _____
4. _____
   _____
   _____
5. _____
   _____
   _____

Daily Goals Sheet   *I can statements for each day.
This is the list of things that I want to accomplish (complete) today in class.

Tasks or assignments I need to complete in class *I can exercise strategies like deep breathing (4-7-8 breathing) to calm or focus myself.	Completed? Check if "yes"
1. Entry journal prompt response & daily gratitude statement *I can recognize what I value and appreciate. *I can write a thoughtful & clear response to a writing prompt.	
2. Daily Goals Sheet filled out *I can plan short-term goals in order to reach my long term goals.	
3. CNN Student News Guided Notes 1-5 *I can summarize events in a news story.	
4. Close Reading/Literacy Activity: Today we are_____ _____ *I can complete a close reading or literacy strategy for something that I read. *I can organize and summarize information.	
Write your own goals for your school work for #s 5 and 6.	
5.	
6. *I can complete activities & lessons in my online courses.	
8. Reflection sheet on goals today	

Created by **Melissa Marini Švigelj-Smith** 2017-2019

*I can reflect on my day and write honestly about whether or not I accomplished my short-term goals.	

In class today, my behavior goals are… Write your own personal goals for #s 3 & 4 *I can use strategies to maintain positive behaviors & reduce negative behaviors.	Did I …? Check if "yes"
1. I will keep a growth mindset.	
2. I will make healthy choices.	
3.	
4.	

DAILY REFLECTION

Explain what you did well today in at least one complete sentence. _____
_____

Explain how you would rate your performance in class today on a scale of 10 to 1, and explain why you ranked yourself that way. 10= I did my best 5= I tried half the time 1=I did not try at all
_____
_____

Write a complete sentence about one part of your work in class that you would like to improve and explain why.
_____
_____

Choose to complete at least ONE of the writing prompts below. Circle which one you are completing.
1. I wish that you would have known today that I…
2. I am really proud that today I…
3. My favorite part of today was…
4. I wonder if today I could...

_____
_____

Created by **Melissa Marini Švigelj-Smith** 2017-2019

Name_____Date_____

Write one thing you are grateful (**thankful**) for today. Finding things to be thankful for helps improve our overall happiness. Happier people are more successful people. _____

_____

I'm thankful to be in class with you today!
Remember to practice 4-7-8 breathing as needed, and to keep a growth mindset.

> **Develop a *GROWTH MINDSET* -** People who believe their talents can be developed (through hard work, good strategies & input from others) have a growth mindset. They tend to achieve more than those with a fixed mindset. ~Dr. Carol Dweck

Instead of thinking...	Try thinking...
I give up	I won't stop until I succeed
I'm not good at this	How can I get better?
I can't be any better	I can always improve
This is too hard	This may take some time
I can't do this	I am going to learn to do this
My mistakes ruined me	I can learn from my mistakes
My plan didn't work	I can try another plan
I'm not smart	I can always learn new things
I'm jealous	I can learn from their success

Belly Breathe with Common and Colbie Callait (2 mins)

1. What do Common and Colbie tell us we can do to calm our "inner monster"?
2. What can help us feel like ourselves again if we are angry?

4 Steps to Developing a Growth Mindset? (4 mins)

List four steps to developing a growth mindset from the video.

1. _____
2. _____
3. _____
4. _____

Am I Not Human? A call for criminal justice reform, Marlon Peterson TEDxTalk (7.5 mins)

1. What did the people in Trinidad/Tobago do with the steel left behind by the US military?
2. Why was Mr. Peterson arrested?
3. What made Mr. Peterson feel relevant while he was incarcerated?
4. What does Mr. Peterson say gun violence visibly displays?
5. Write one thing you heard Mr. Peterson ask listeners to do.

CNN 10 STUDENT NEWS (10 minute show) *Write 5 things you learn from the news today.*

1. _____
2. _____
3. _____
4. _____
5. _____

Daily Goals Sheet *I can statements for each day.
This is the list of things that I want to accomplish (complete) today in class.

Tasks or assignments I need to complete in class *I can exercise strategies like deep breathing (4-7-8 breathing) to calm or focus myself.	Completed? Check if "yes"
1. Entry journal prompt response & daily gratitude statement *I can recognize what I value and appreciate. *I can write a thoughtful & clear response to a writing prompt.	
2. Daily Goals Sheet filled out *I can plan short-term goals in order to reach my long term goals.	
3. CNN Student News Guided Notes 1-5 *I can summarize events in a news story.	
4. Close Reading/Literacy Activity: Today we are_____ *I can complete a close reading or literacy strategy for something that I read. *I can organize and summarize information.	
Write your own goals for your school work for #s 5 and 6.	

Created by **Melissa Marini Švigelj-Smith** 2017-2019

5.	
6. *I can complete activities & lessons in my courses.	
7. Reflection sheet on goals today *I can reflect on my day and write honestly about whether or not I accomplished my short-term goals.	

In class today, my behavior goals are… **Write your own personal goals for #s 3 & 4** *I can use strategies to maintain positive behaviors & reduce negative behaviors.	Did I …? Check if "yes"
1. I will keep a growth mindset.	
2. I will make healthy choices.	
3.	
4.	

DAILY REFLECTION

Explain what you did well today in at least one complete sentence

_____
_____

Explain how you would rate your performance in class today on a scale of 10 to 1, and explain why you ranked yourself that way. 10= I did my best 5= I tried half the time 1=I did not try at all

_____
_____
_____

Write a complete sentence about one part of your work in class that you would like to improve and explain why._____

_____

Choose to complete at least ONE of the writing prompts below. Circle which one you are completing.
1. I wish that you would have known today that I…
2. I am really proud that today I…
3. My favorite part of today was…
4. I wonder if today I could…

_____
_____
_____

Name_____ Date_____

Write one thing you are grateful (**thankful**) for today. Finding things to be thankful for helps improve our overall happiness. Happier people are more successful people._____
_____

I'm grateful for wise words from those with experience.
Remember to practice 4-7-8 breathing as needed, and to keep a growth mindset.

> **Develop a GROWTH MINDSET -** *People who believe their talents can be developed (through hard work, good strategies & input from others) have a growth mindset. They tend to achieve more than those with a fixed mindset. ~Dr. Carol Dweck*

Instead of thinking...	Try thinking...
I give up	I won't stop until I succeed
I'm not good at this	How can I get better?
I can't be any better	I can always improve
This is too hard	This may take some time
I can't do this	I am going to learn to do this
My mistakes ruined me	I can learn from my mistakes
My plan didn't work	I can try another plan
I'm not smart	I can always learn new things
I'm jealous	I can learn from their success

Bruce Talks Candidly About His Time in Prison and Life on the Streets | Released | OWN
(4.5 minutes)

1. What is one reason Bruce said he "took to the streets?"

2. Why did Bruce say he targeted drug dealers?

3. What did Bruce say was one of his worst experiences in prison?

4. What did Bruce say he would've done differently now that he looks back?

CNN 10 STUDENT NEWS **(10 minute show)** *Write 5 things you learned from the news today.*

1. _____
   _____
2. _____
   _____
3. _____
   _____
4. _____
   _____
5. _____
   _____

Daily Goals Sheet   **I can statements for each day.*
This is the list of things that I want to accomplish (complete) today in class.

Tasks or assignments I need to complete in class *I can exercise strategies like deep breathing (4-7-8 breathing) to calm or focus myself.	Completed? Check if "yes"
1. Entry journal prompt response & daily gratitude statement *I can recognize what I value and appreciate. *I can write a thoughtful & clear response to a writing prompt.	
2. Daily Goals Sheet filled out *I can plan short-term goals in order to reach my long term goals.	
3. CNN Student News Guided Notes 1-5 *I can summarize events in a news story.	
4. Close Reading/Literacy Activity: Today we are_____ _____ *I can complete a close reading or literacy strategy for something that I read. *I can organize and summarize information.	
Write your own goals for your school work for #s 5 and 6.	
5.	
6. *I can complete activities & lessons in my courses.	
7. Reflection sheet on goals today	

Created by **Melissa Marini Švigelj-Smith** 2017-2019

*I can reflect on my day and write honestly about whether or not I accomplished my short-term goals.	

In class today, my behavior goals are… Write your own personal goals for #s 3 & 4 *I can use strategies to maintain positive behaviors & reduce negative behaviors.	Did I …? Check if "yes"
1. I will keep a growth mindset.	
2. I will make healthy choices.	
3.	
4.	

DAILY REFLECTION

Explain what you did well today in at least one complete sentence
_____
_____

Explain how you would rate your performance in class today on a scale of 10 to 1, and explain why you ranked yourself that way. 10= I did my best 5= I tried half the time 1=I did not try at all
_____
_____
_____

Write a complete sentence about one part of your work in class that you would like to improve and explain why._____
_____
_____

Choose to complete at least ONE of the writing prompts below. Circle which one you are completing.
1. I wish that you would have known today that I…
2. I am really proud that today I…
3. My favorite part of today was…
4. I wonder if today I could…

_____
_____
_____

Name_____ Date_____

Write one thing you are grateful (**thankful**) for today. Finding things to be thankful for helps improve our overall happiness. Happier people are more successful people._____

_____

Today I am thankful for my elders.

Remember to practice 4-7-8 breathing as needed, and to keep a growth mindset.

> **Develop a GROWTH MINDSET -** *People who believe their talents can be developed (through hard work, good strategies & input from others) have a growth mindset. They tend to achieve more than those with a fixed mindset. ~Dr. Carol Dweck*

Instead of thinking...	Try thinking...
I give up	I won't stop until I succeed
I'm not good at this	How can I get better?
I can't be any better	I can always improve
This is too hard	This may take some time
I can't do this	I am going to learn to do this
My mistakes ruined me	I can learn from my mistakes
My plan didn't work	I can try another plan
I'm not smart	I can always learn new things
I'm jealous	I can learn from their success

4-7-8 Breathing
Use this strategy to help you stay calm & to relax
4 - Breathe in as you count to 4
7 - Hold your breath as you count to 7
8 - Breathe out as you count to 8

~Dr. Andrew Weil

[Bryan Stevenson: We Need to Talk About an Injustice](#) TED Talk (24 minutes)

1. What did Bryan learn from his grandmother?

2. What did Bryan learn from his brother?

3. What percentage of African American men in Alabama have lost their right to vote?

4. How many people out of 9 people on death row have been exonerated?

5. What are Americans unwilling to commit to or face as a collective whole?

6. What did Rosa Parks tell Mr. Stevenson that he was going to be?

7. What is the opposite of poverty according to the speaker?

8. What did the older African American gentleman tell Mr. Stevenson?

Created by **Melissa Marini Švigelj-Smith** 2017-2019

[CNN 10 STUDENT NEWS](#) (10 minute show)
Write 5 things you learned from the news today.

1. _____
   _____
   _____
2. _____
   _____
   _____
3. _____
   _____
   _____
4. _____
   _____
   _____
5. _____
   _____
   _____

Daily Goals Sheet   **I can statements for each day.*
This is the list of things that I want to accomplish (complete) today in class.

Tasks or assignments I need to complete in class *I can exercise strategies like deep breathing (4-7-8 breathing) to calm or focus myself.	Completed? Check if "yes"
1. Entry journal prompt response & daily gratitude statement *I can recognize what I value and appreciate. *I can write a thoughtful & clear response to a writing prompt.	
2. Daily Goals Sheet filled out *I can plan short-term goals in order to reach my long term goals.	
3. CNN Student News Guided Notes 1-5 *I can summarize events in a news story.	
4. Close Reading/Literacy Activity: Today we are_____ _____ *I can complete a close reading or literacy strategy for something that I read. *I can organize and summarize information.	
Write your own goals for your school work for #s 5 and 6.	
5.	
6. *I can complete activities & lessons in my courses.	

Created by **Melissa Marini Švigelj-Smith** 2017-2019

7. Reflection sheet on goals today *I can reflect on my day and write honestly about whether or not I accomplished my short-term goals.	

In class today, my behavior goals are… Write your own personal goals for #s 3 & 4 *I can use strategies to maintain positive behaviors & reduce negative behaviors.	Did I …? Check if "yes"
1. I will keep a growth mindset.	
2. I will make healthy choices.	
3.	
4.	

DAILY REFLECTION

Explain what you did well today in at least one complete sentence. _____
_____

Explain how you would rate your performance in class today on a scale of 10 to 1, and explain why you ranked yourself that way. 10= I did my best 5= I tried half the time 1=I did not try at all
_____
_____
_____

Write a complete sentence about one part of your work in class that you would like to improve and explain why.
_____
_____
_____

Choose to complete at least ONE of the writing prompts below. Circle which one you are completing.
1. I wish that you would have known today that I…
2. I am really proud that today I…
3. My favorite part of today was…
4. I wonder if today I could...

_____
_____
_____

Name_____ Date_____

Write one thing you are grateful (**thankful**) for today. Finding things to be thankful for helps improve our overall happiness. Happier people are more successful people. _____
_____

Develop a GROWTH MINDSET - People who believe their talents can be developed (through hard work, good strategies & input from others) have a growth mindset. They tend to achieve more than those with a fixed mindset. ~Dr. Carol Dweck

---

Instead of thinking...	Try thinking...
I give up	I won't stop until I succeed
I'm not good at this	How can I get better?
I can't be any better	I can always improve
This is too hard	This may take some time
I can't do this	I am going to learn to do this
My mistakes ruined me	I can learn from my mistakes
My plan didn't work	I can try another plan
I'm not smart	I can always learn new things
I'm jealous	I can learn from their success

4-7-8 Breathing
Use this strategy to help you stay calm & to relax
4 - Breathe in as you count to 4
7 - Hold your breath as you count to 7
8 - Breathe out as you count to 8

~Dr. Andrew Weil

Remember to practice 4-7-8 Breathing to assist with staying calm and focused and keep a growth mindset.

Carry On - ESPN - http://www.espn.com/espn/otl/story/_/id/9454322/why-stayed
(21 minutes)

1. Which city does this story take place in?

2. What is a challenge that Dartanyon faced as a young man?

3. What is a challenge that Leroy faced as a young man?

4. How did strangers help out the young men?

5. What did Lisa Fenn say she learned from Leroy and Dartanyon?

6. What does Dartanyon call Lisa to tell her?

7. How does Dartanyon feel about his experiences with Lisa Fenn?

Created by **Melissa Marini Švigelj-Smith** 2017-2019

Daily Goals Sheet *I can statements for each day.
This is the list of things that I want to accomplish (complete) today in class.

Tasks or assignments I need to complete in class *I can exercise strategies like deep breathing (4-7-8 breathing) to calm or focus myself.	Completed? Check if "yes"
1. Entry journal prompt response & daily gratitude statement *I can recognize what I value and appreciate. *I can write a thoughtful & clear response to a writing prompt.	
2. Daily Goals Sheet filled out *I can plan short-term goals in order to reach my long term goals.	
3. CNN Student News Guided Notes 1-5 *I can summarize events in a news story.	
4. Close Reading/Literacy Activity: Today we are_____ _____ *I can complete a close reading or literacy strategy for something that I read. *I can organize and summarize information.	
Write your own goals for your school work for #s 5 and 6.	
5.	
6. *I can complete activities & lessons in my courses.	
7. Reflection sheet on goals today *I can reflect on my day and write honestly about whether or not I accomplished my short-term goals.	

In class today, my behavior goals are… Write your own personal goals for #s 3 & 4 *I can use strategies to maintain positive behaviors & reduce negative behaviors.	Did I …? Check if "yes"
1. I will keep a growth mindset.	
2. I will make healthy choices.	
3.	
4.	

Created by Melissa Marini Švigelj-Smith 2017-2019

DAILY REFLECTION

Explain what you did well today in at least one complete sentence.
_____
_____

Explain how you would rate your performance in class today on a scale of 10 to 1, and explain why you ranked yourself that way. 10= I did my best 5= I tried half the time 1=I did not try at all
_____
_____

Write a complete sentence about one part of your work in class that you would like to improve and explain why.
_____
_____

Choose to complete ONE of the writing prompts below. Circle which one you are completing.
1. I wish that you would have known today that I…
2. I am really proud that today I…
3. My favorite part of today was…
4. I wonder if today I could...

_____
_____
_____

Name_____ Date_____

Write one thing you are grateful (**thankful**) for today. Finding things to be thankful for helps improve our overall happiness. Happier people are more successful people._____

_____

Today I am thankful for games to play.
Remember to practice 4-7-8 breathing as needed, and to keep a growth mindset.

Develop a GROWTH MINDSET - *People who believe their talents can be developed (through hard work, good strategies & input from others) have a growth mindset. They tend to achieve more than those with a fixed mindset. ~Dr. Carol Dweck*

Instead of thinking...	Try thinking...
I give up	I won't stop until I succeed
I'm not good at this	How can I get better?
I can't be any better	I can always improve
This is too hard	This may take some time
I can't do this	I am going to learn to do this
My mistakes ruined me	I can learn from my mistakes
My plan didn't work	I can try another plan
I'm not smart	I can always learn new things
I'm jealous	I can learn from their success

Chess and Community: the power of a single hour/Lemuel LaRoche TEDTalk (16 minutes)

1. What was Mr. LaRoche's degree in?

2. What did Mr. LaRoche walk away with, even though he lost his chess match while overseas?

3. Mr. LaRoche said he wants young people to know the difference between reacting and _____.

4. Don't be used as a _____ (one of the chess pieces/4-letter word).

5. What might the queen chess piece represent according to Mr. LaRoche?

Created by **Melissa Marini Švigelj-Smith** 2017-2019

6. How many hours are in a month?

7. What is another activity that chess led to?

8. We all possess the power to change the _____.

9. What is the tone (attitude) of the poem?

10. What is the theme (message) of the poem?

CNN 10 STUDENT NEWS (10 minute show)
Write 5 things you learned from the news today.

1. _____
2. _____
3. _____
4. _____
5. _____

Daily Goals Sheet *I can statements for each day.*
This is the list of things that I want to accomplish (complete) today in class.

Tasks or assignments I need to complete in class *I can exercise strategies like deep breathing (4-7-8 breathing) to calm or focus myself.	Completed? Check if "yes"
1. Entry journal prompt response & daily gratitude statement *I can recognize what I value and appreciate. *I can write a thoughtful & clear response to a writing prompt.	
2. Daily Goals Sheet filled out *I can plan short-term goals in order to reach my long term goals.	
3. CNN Student News Guided Notes 1-5 *I can summarize events in a news story.	
4. Close Reading/Literacy Activity: Today we are_____ _____ *I can complete a close reading or literacy strategy for something that I read. *I can organize and summarize information.	

Created by **Melissa Marini Švigelj-Smith** 2017-2019

Write your own goals for your school work for #s 5 and 6.	
5.	
6. *I can complete activities & lessons in my courses.	
7. Reflection sheet on goals today *I can reflect on my day and write honestly about whether or not I accomplished my short-term goals.	

In class today, my behavior goals are… Write your own personal goals for #s 3 & 4 *I can use strategies to maintain positive behaviors & reduce negative behaviors.	Did I …? Check if "yes"
1. I will keep a growth mindset.	
2. I will make healthy choices.	
3.	
4.	

DAILY REFLECTION

Explain what you did well today in at least one complete sentence. _____

_____

Explain how you would rate your performance in class today on a scale of 10 to 1, and explain why you ranked yourself that way. 10= I did my best 5= I tried half the time 1=I did not try at all

_____

_____

Write a complete sentence about one part of your work in class that you would like to improve and explain why.

_____

_____

Choose to complete at least ONE of the writing prompts below. Circle which one you are completing.
1. I wish you would have known today that I…
2. I am really proud that today I…
3. My favorite part of today was…
4. I wonder if today I could...

_____

_____

Created by **Melissa Marini Švigelj-Smith** 2017-2019

Name_____ Date_____

Write one thing you are grateful (**thankful**) for today. Finding things to be thankful for helps improve our overall happiness. Happier people are more successful people._____
_____

Today I am thankful for leaders and followers.
Remember to practice 4-7-8 breathing as needed, and to keep a growth mindset.

Develop a *GROWTH MINDSET* - People who believe their talents can be developed (through hard work, good strategies & input from others) have a growth mindset. They tend to achieve more than those with a fixed mindset. ~Dr. Carol Dweck

Instead of thinking...	Try thinking...
I give up	I won't stop until I succeed
I'm not good at this	How can I get better?
I can't be any better	I can always improve
This is too hard	This may take some time
I can't do this	I am going to learn to do this
My mistakes ruined me	I can learn from my mistakes
My plan didn't work	I can try another plan
I'm not smart	I can always learn new things
I'm jealous	I can learn from their success

4-7-8 Breathing
Use this strategy to help you stay calm & to relax
4 - Breathe in as you count to 4
7 - Hold your breath as you count to 7
8 - Breathe out as you count to 8

~Dr. Andrew Weil

[Clint Smith: The Danger of Silence](#) **TED Talk (4 minutes)**

0:12 Dr. Martin Luther King, Jr., in a 1968 speech where he reflects upon the Civil Rights Movement, states, "In the end, we will remember not the words of our enemies but the silence of our friends."
1. What did Dr. King mean by the statement underlined? _____
_____

2. Highlight or underline Mr. Smith's 4 core principles in his classroom.

0:26 As a teacher, I've internalized this message. Every day, all around us, we see the consequences of silence manifest themselves in the form of discrimination, violence, genocide and war. In the classroom, I challenge my students to explore the silences in their own lives through poetry. We work together to fill those spaces, to recognize them, to name them, to understand that they don't have to be sources of shame. In an effort to create a culture within my classroom where students feel safe sharing the intimacies of their own silences, I have four core principles posted on

Created by **Melissa Marini Švigelj-Smith** 2017-2019

the board that sits in the front of my class, which every student signs at the beginning of the year: read critically, write consciously, speak clearly, tell your truth.

1:13 And I find myself thinking a lot about that last point, tell your truth. And I realized that if I was going to ask my students to speak up, I was going to have to tell my truth and be honest with them about the times where I failed to do so.

3. Highlight or underline a time that Mr. Smith failed to use his voice and speak up.

1:27 So I tell them that growing up, as a kid in a Catholic family in New Orleans, during Lent I was always taught that the most meaningful thing one could do was to give something up, sacrifice something you typically indulge in to prove to God you understand his sanctity. I've given up soda, McDonald's, French fries, French kisses, and everything in between. But one year, I gave up speaking. I figured the most valuable thing I could sacrifice was my own voice, but it was like I hadn't realized that I had given that up a long time ago. I spent so much of my life telling people the things they wanted to hear instead of the things they needed to, told myself I wasn't meant to be anyone's conscience because I still had to figure out being my own, so sometimes I just wouldn't say anything, appeasing ignorance with my silence, unaware that validation doesn't need words to endorse its existence. When Christian was beat up for being gay, I put my hands in my pocket and walked with my head down as if I didn't even notice. I couldn't use my locker for weeks because the bolt on the lock reminded me of the one I had put on my lips when the homeless man on the corner looked at me with eyes up merely searching for an affirmation that he was worth seeing. I was more concerned with touching the screen on my Apple than actually feeding him one. When the woman at the fundraising gala said "I'm so proud of you. It must be so hard teaching those poor, unintelligent kids," I bit my lip, because apparently we needed her money more than my students needed their dignity.

4. What is the tone or mood of the following paragraph? Highlight or underline evidence (words) from the text (reading) to prove what the mood or tone is in the paragraph.

_____

_____

2:52 We spend so much time listening to the things people are saying that we rarely pay attention to the things they don't. Silence is the residue of fear. It is feeling your flaws gut-wrench guillotine your tongue. It is the air retreating from your chest because it doesn't feel safe in your lungs. Silence is Rwandan genocide. Silence is Katrina. It is what you hear when there aren't enough body bags left. It is the sound after the noose is already tied. It is charring. It is chains. It is privilege. It is pain. There is no time to pick your battles when your battles have already picked you

5. Highlight or underline ways that Mr. Smith is going to use his voice to be an upstander and fight injustice or unkindness. .

3:27 I will not let silence wrap itself around my indecision. I will tell Christian that he is a lion, a sanctuary of bravery and brilliance. I will ask that homeless man what his name is and how his day was, because sometimes all people want to be is human. I will tell that woman that my students can talk about transcendentalism like their last name was Thoreau, and just because you watched one episode of "The Wire" doesn't mean you know anything about my kids. So this year, instead of giving something up, I will live everyday as if there were a microphone tucked under my tongue, a stage on the underside of my inhibition. Because who has to have a soapbox when all you've ever needed is your voice?

CNN 10 STUDENT NEWS (10 minute show)
Write 5 things you learned from the news today.

1. _____
   _____
   _____

2. _____
   _____
   _____

3. _____
   _____
   _____

4. _____
   _____
   _____

5. _____
   _____
   _____

Daily Goals Sheet   **I can statements for each day.*
This is the list of things that I want to accomplish (complete) today in class.

Tasks or assignments I need to complete in class	Completed? Check if "yes"
*I can exercise strategies like deep breathing (4-7-8 breathing) to calm or focus myself.	
1. Entry journal prompt response & daily gratitude statement *I can recognize what I value and appreciate. *I can write a thoughtful & clear response to a writing prompt.	
2. Daily Goals Sheet filled out *I can plan short-term goals in order to reach my long term goals.	
3. CNN Student News Guided Notes 1-5 *I can summarize events in a news story.	
4. Close Reading/Literacy Activity: Today we are_____ *I can complete a close reading or literacy strategy for something that I read. *I can organize and summarize information.	
Write your own goals for your school work for #s 5 and 6.	
5.	
6.	

Created by **Melissa Marini Švigelj-Smith** 2017-2019

*I can complete activities & lessons in my courses.	
7. Reflection sheet on goals today *I can reflect on my day and write honestly about whether or not I accomplished my short-term goals.	

In class today, my behavior goals are… Write your own personal goals for #s 3 & 4 *I can use strategies to maintain positive behaviors & reduce negative behaviors.	Did I …? Check if "yes"
1. I will keep a growth mindset.	
2. I will make healthy choices.	
3.	
4.	

DAILY REFLECTION

Explain what you did well today in at least one complete sentence. _____
_____

Explain how you would rate your performance in class today on a scale of 10 to 1, and explain why you ranked yourself that way. 10= I did my best 5= I tried half the time 1=I did not try at all
_____
_____

Write a complete sentence about one part of your work in class you would like to improve and explain why.
_____
_____

Choose to complete at least ONE of the writing prompts below. Circle which one you are completing.
1. I wish you would have known today that I…
2. I am really proud that today I…
3. My favorite part of today was…
4. I wonder if today I could...

_____
_____
_____

Name_____ Date_____

Write one thing you are grateful (**thankful**) for today. Finding things to be thankful for helps improve our overall happiness. Happier people are more successful people._____
_____

Today, I am thankful I have students who are polite and courteous.
Remember to practice 4-7-8 breathing as needed, and to keep a growth mindset.

> **Develop a GROWTH MINDSET -** *People who believe their talents can be developed (through hard work, good strategies & input from others) have a growth mindset. They tend to achieve more than those with a fixed mindset. ~Dr. Carol Dweck*

Instead of thinking...	Try thinking...
I give up	I won't stop until I succeed
I'm not good at this	How can I get better?
I can't be any better	I can always improve
This is too hard	This may take some time
I can't do this	I am going to learn to do this
My mistakes ruined me	I can learn from my mistakes
My plan didn't work	I can try another plan
I'm not smart	I can always learn new things
I'm jealous	I can learn from their success

4-7-8 Breathing
Use this strategy to help you stay calm & to relax
4 - Breathe in as you count to 4
7 - Hold your breath as you count to 7
8 - Breathe out as you count to 8

~Dr. Andrew Weil

TED Talk **Dan Gross: Why Gun Violence Can't Be Our New Normal** (13:39 mins)

1. What event caused a change in Dan's life in 1997?
2. Why did Dan quit his job in advertising?
3. What policy does most of the American public agree about with regard to guns?
4. Why do millions of Americans incorrectly believe that having a gun at home makes them safer?
5. What is the "bold goal" of the Brady Campaign?
6. According to Dan, what does it usually take to wake Congress up when they're on the wrong side of history?
7. Name a behavior in our society/culture in the past that is now less common and considered unhealthy.
8. What is Dan's hope for future generations in our country?

CNN 10 STUDENT NEWS (10 minute show)
Write 5 things you learned from the news today.

1. _____
   _____
   _____
2. _____
   _____
   _____
3. _____
   _____
   _____
4. _____
   _____
   _____
5. _____
   _____
   _____

Daily Goals Sheet *I can statements for each day.
This is the list of things that I want to accomplish (complete) today in class.

Tasks or assignments I need to complete in class *I can exercise strategies like deep breathing (4-7-8 breathing) to calm or focus myself.	Completed? Check if "yes"
1. Entry journal prompt response & daily gratitude statement *I can recognize what I value and appreciate. *I can write a thoughtful & clear response to a writing prompt.	
2. Daily Goals Sheet filled out *I can plan short-term goals in order to reach my long term goals.	
3. CNN Student News Guided Notes 1-5 *I can summarize events in a news story.	
4. Close Reading/Literacy Activity: Today we are_____ _____ *I can complete a close reading or literacy strategy for something that I read. *I can organize and summarize information.	
Write your own goals for your school work for #s 5 and 6.	
5.	
6. *I can complete activities & lessons in my courses.	
7. Reflection sheet on goals today	

*I can reflect on my day and write honestly about whether or not I accomplished my short-term goals.	

In class today, my behavior goals are… **Write your own personal goals for #s 3 & 4** *I can use strategies to maintain positive behaviors & reduce negative behaviors.	Did I …? Check if "yes"
1. I will keep a growth mindset.	
2. I will make healthy choices.	
3.	
4.	

DAILY REFLECTION

Explain what you did well today in at least one complete sentence. _____
_____

Explain how you would rate your performance in class today on a scale of 10 to 1, and explain why you ranked yourself that way. 10= I did my best 5= I tried half the time 1=I did not try at all
_____
_____

Write a complete sentence about one part of your work in class that you would like to improve and explain why.
_____
_____

Choose to complete at least ONE of the writing prompts below. Circle which one you are completing.
1. I wish that you would have known today that I…
2. I am really proud that today I…
3. My favorite part of today was…
4. I wonder if today I could...
_____
_____
_____

Created by **Melissa Marini Švigelj-Smith** 2017-2019

Name_____ Date_____

Write one thing you are grateful (**thankful**) for today. Finding things to be thankful for helps improve our overall happiness. Happier people are more successful people._____
_____

Today I am thankful for people who recycle.
Remember to practice 4-7-8 breathing as needed, and to keep a growth mindset.

> **Develop a** *GROWTH MINDSET* **-** People who believe their talents can be developed (through hard work, good strategies & input from others) have a growth mindset. They tend to achieve more than those with a fixed mindset. ~Dr. Carol Dweck

Instead of thinking...	Try thinking...
I give up	I won't stop until I succeed
I'm not good at this	How can I get better?
I can't be any better	I can always improve
This is too hard	This may take some time
I can't do this	I am going to learn to do this
My mistakes ruined me	I can learn from my mistakes
My plan didn't work	I can try another plan
I'm not smart	I can always learn new things
I'm jealous	I can learn from their success

~Dr. Andrew Weil

TED Talk Dan Phillips: Creative houses from reclaimed stuff
(18 minutes)

1. - 3. Name 3 things Dan used to make something in or as part of his houses.

4. Which mindset creates a lot of waste? (Dionysian or Apollonian)

5. What does Jean-Paul Sartre's "the divided self" theory mean?

6. Why is it okay to have failures?

CNN 10 STUDENT NEWS (10 minute show)

*Write **5** things you learned from the news today.*

1. _____
_____
_____

2. _____
_____
_____

3. _____
_____
_____

4. _____
_____
_____

5. _____
_____
_____

Daily Goals Sheet *I can statements for each day.

This is the list of things that I want to accomplish (complete) today in class.

Tasks or assignments I need to complete in class *I can exercise strategies like deep breathing (4-7-8 breathing) to calm or focus myself.	Completed? Check if "yes"
1. Entry journal prompt response & daily gratitude statement *I can recognize what I value and appreciate. *I can write a thoughtful & clear response to a writing prompt.	
2. Daily Goals Sheet filled out *I can plan short-term goals in order to reach my long term goals.	
3. CNN Student News Guided Notes 1-5 *I can summarize events in a news story.	
4. Close Reading/Literacy Activity: Today we are_____ *I can complete a close reading or literacy strategy for something that I read. *I can organize and summarize information.	
Write your own goals for your school work for #s 5 and 6.	
5.	
6. *I can complete activities & lessons in my courses.	

Created by **Melissa Marini Švigelj-Smith** 2017-2019

| 7. Reflection sheet on goals today
*I can reflect on my day and write honestly about whether or not I accomplished my short-term goals. | |

In class today, my behavior goals are… Write your own personal goals for #s 3 & 4 *I can use strategies to maintain positive behaviors & reduce negative behaviors.	Did I …? Check if "yes"
1. I will keep a growth mindset.	
2. I will make healthy choices.	
3.	
4.	

DAILY REFLECTION

Explain what you did well today in at least one complete sentence. _____
_____

Explain how you would rate your performance in class today on a scale of 10 to 1, and explain why you ranked yourself that way. 10= I did my best 5= I tried half the time 1=I did not try at all
_____
_____

Write a complete sentence about one part of your work in class you would like to improve and explain why.
_____
_____

Choose to complete at least ONE of the writing prompts below. Circle which one you are completing.
1. I wish you would have known today that I…
2. I am really proud that today I…
3. My favorite part of today was…
4. I wonder if today I could...

_____
_____
_____

Created by **Melissa Marini Švigelj-Smith** 2017-2019

Name_____Date_____

Write one thing you are grateful (**thankful**) for today. Finding things to be thankful for helps improve our overall happiness. Happier people are more successful people._____
_____

I am thankful for our amazing brains!
Remember to practice 4-7-8 breathing as needed and to keep a growth mindset.

> **Develop a *GROWTH MINDSET* -** *People who believe their talents can be developed (through hard work, good strategies & input from others) have a growth mindset. They tend to achieve more than those with a fixed mindset. ~Dr. Carol Dweck*

Instead of thinking...	Try thinking...
I give up	I won't stop until I succeed
I'm not good at this	How can I get better?
I can't be any better	I can always improve
This is too hard	This may take some time
I can't do this	I am going to learn to do this
My mistakes ruined me	I can learn from my mistakes
My plan didn't work	I can try another plan
I'm not smart	I can always learn new things
I'm jealous	I can learn from their success

Dare to Dream Again, Prophet Walker TED Talk (6 minutes)

1. What did Prophet say helped him "dream beyond the bars?"

2. What does Prophet say is a simple right denied to many children?

3. What does Prophet say that he is paid to do?

4. What does Prophet say everyone is obligated to do for all of us and our children?

5. Who is the person that Prophet quotes at the end of his talk?

CNN 10 STUDENT NEWS (10 minute show) *Write 5 things you learned from the news today.*

1. _____
_____
2. _____
_____
3. _____
_____
4. _____
_____
5. _____
_____

Daily Goals Sheet *****I can statements for each day.**
This is the list of things that I want to accomplish (complete) today in class.

Tasks or assignments I need to complete in class *I can exercise strategies like deep breathing (4-7-8 breathing) to calm or focus myself.	Completed? Check if "yes"
1. Entry journal prompt response & daily gratitude statement *I can recognize what I value and appreciate. *I can write a thoughtful & clear response to a writing prompt.	
2. Daily Goals Sheet filled out *I can plan short-term goals in order to reach my long term goals.	
3. CNN Student News Guided Notes 1-5 *I can summarize events in a news story.	
4. Close Reading/Literacy Activity: Today we are_____ _____ *I can complete a close reading or literacy strategy for something that I read. *I can organize and summarize information.	
Write your own goals for your school work for #s 6 and 7.	
5.	
6. *I can complete activities & lessons in my courses.	
7. Reflection sheet on goals today *I can reflect on my day and write honestly about whether or not I	

Created by **Melissa Marini Švigelj-Smith** 2017-2019

accomplished my short-term goals.	

In class today, my behavior goals are… Write your own personal goals for #s 3 & 4 *I can use strategies to maintain positive behaviors & reduce negative behaviors.	Did I …? Check if "yes"
1. I will keep a growth mindset.	
2. I will make healthy choices.	
3.	
4.	

DAILY REFLECTION
Explain what you did well today in at least one complete sentence
_____
_____

Explain how you would rate your performance in class today on a scale of 10 to 1, and explain why you ranked yourself that way. 10= I did my best 5= I tried half the time 1=I did not try at all
_____
_____
_____

Write a complete sentence about one part of your work in class you would like to improve and explain why._____
_____
_____

Choose to complete ONE of the writing prompts below. Circle which one you are completing.
1. I wish you would have known today that I…
2. I am really proud that today I…
3. My favorite part of today was…
4. I wonder if today I could…

_____
_____
_____

Created by **Melissa Marini Švigelj-Smith** 2017-2019

Name_____ Date_____

Write one thing you are grateful (**thankful**) for today. Finding things to be thankful for helps improve our overall happiness. Happier people are more successful people._____

_____

Today I am thankful for new discoveries.

Remember to practice 4-7-8 breathing as needed and to keep a growth mindset.

> **Develop a GROWTH MINDSET -** *People who believe their talents can be developed (through hard work, good strategies & input from others) have a growth mindset. They tend to achieve more than those with a fixed mindset. ~Dr. Carol Dweck*

Instead of thinking...	Try thinking...
I give up	I won't stop until I succeed
I'm not good at this	How can I get better?
I can't be any better	I can always improve
This is too hard	This may take some time
I can't do this	I am going to learn to do this
My mistakes ruined me	I can learn from my mistakes
My plan didn't work	I can try another plan
I'm not smart	I can always learn new things
I'm jealous	I can learn from their success

4-7-8 Breathing
Use this strategy to help you stay calm & to relax
4 - Breathe in as you count to 4
7 - Hold your breath as you count to 7
8 - Breathe out as you count to 8

~Dr. Andrew Weil

[David Gallo: Underwater astonishments](#) **(5 minutes) TED Talk**

1. What are some things deepwater creatures can create with neon color?

2. Describe how a cephalopod can change to match the environment.

3. & 4. What are 2 things an octopus can change to match his surroundings?

Created by **Melissa Marini Švigelj-Smith** 2017-2019

CNN 10 STUDENT NEWS (10 minute show)
Write 5 things you learned from the news today.

1. _____
   _____
2. _____
   _____
3. _____
   _____
4. _____
   _____
5. _____
   _____

Daily Goals Sheet   **I can statements for each day.*

This is the list of things that I want to accomplish (complete) today in class.

Tasks or assignments I need to complete in class *I can exercise strategies like deep breathing (4-7-8 breathing) to calm or focus myself.	Completed? Check if "yes"
1. Entry journal prompt response & daily gratitude statement *I can recognize what I value and appreciate. *I can write a thoughtful & clear response to a writing prompt.	
2. Daily Goals Sheet filled out *I can plan short-term goals in order to reach my long term goals.	
3. CNN Student News Guided Notes 1-5 *I can summarize events in a news story.	
4. Close Reading/Literacy Activity: Today we are_____ _____ *I can complete a close reading or literacy strategy for something that I read. *I can organize and summarize information.	
Write your own goals for your school work for #s 5 and 6.	
5.	
6. *I can complete activities & lessons in my courses.	
7. Reflection sheet on goals today	

Created by **Melissa Marini Švigelj-Smith** 2017-2019

*I can reflect on my day and write honestly about whether or not I accomplished my short-term goals.	

In class today, my behavior goals are… Write your own personal goals for #s 3 & 4 *I can use strategies to maintain positive behaviors & reduce negative behaviors.	Did I …? Check if "yes"
1. I will keep a growth mindset.	
2. I will make healthy choices.	
3.	
4.	

DAILY REFLECTION

Explain what you did well today in at least one complete sentence. _____
_____
_____

Explain how you would rate your performance in class today on a scale of 10 to 1, and explain why you ranked yourself that way. 10= I did my best 5= I tried half the time 1=I did not try at all
_____
_____
_____

Write a complete sentence about one part of your work in class you would like to improve and explain why.
_____
_____
_____

Choose to complete at least ONE of the writing prompts below. Circle which one you are completing.
1. I wish you would have known today that I…
2. I am really proud that today I…
3. My favorite part of today was…
4. I wonder if today I could...

_____
_____
_____

Name_____Date_____

Write one thing you are grateful **(thankful)** for today. Finding things to be thankful for helps improve our overall happiness. Happier people are more successful people._____
_____

Today I am thankful to be able to learn about history.
Remember to practice 4-7-8 breathing as needed, and to keep a growth mindset.

> **Develop a *GROWTH MINDSET* -** People who believe their talents can be developed (through hard work, good strategies & input from others) have a growth mindset. They tend to achieve more than those with a fixed mindset. ~Dr. Carol Dweck

Instead of thinking...	Try thinking...
I give up	I won't stop until I succeed
I'm not good at this	How can I get better?
I can't be any better	I can always improve
This is too hard	This may take some time
I can't do this	I am going to learn to do this
My mistakes ruined me	I can learn from my mistakes
My plan didn't work	I can try another plan
I'm not smart	I can always learn new things
I'm jealous	I can learn from their success

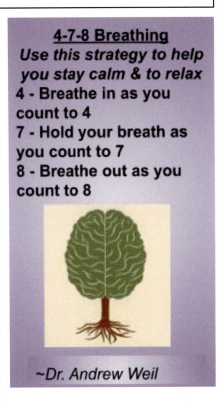

Epigenetics and the Influence of Our Genes - Courtney Griffins TEDx (18 minutes)

1. How many cells are in our bodies?
2. What is chromatin?
3. What actions can affect a developing fetus in a mother's womb?
4. What are long term consequences for children whose mothers' smoked or didn't eat healthy during their pregnancies?
5. How can what someone does in their youth affect their offspring and future generations?
6. What are tumor suppressor genes?
7. How is the approach to treating cancer described, a different approach than one previously used?
8. How can we treat our epigenomes positively?

Created by **Melissa Marini Švigelj-Smith** 2017-2019

CNN 10 STUDENT NEWS (10 minute show)
Write 5 things you learned from the news today.

1. _____
   _____
   _____
2. _____
   _____
   _____
3. _____
   _____
   _____
4. _____
   _____
   _____
5. _____
   _____
   _____

Daily Goals Sheet   *****I can statements for each day.**
This is the list of things that I want to accomplish (complete) today in class.

Tasks or assignments I need to complete in class *I can exercise strategies like deep breathing (4-7-8 breathing) to calm or focus myself.	Completed? Check if "yes"
1. Entry journal prompt response & daily gratitude statement *I can recognize what I value and appreciate. *I can write a thoughtful & clear response to a writing prompt.	
2. Daily Goals Sheet filled out *I can plan short-term goals in order to reach my long term goals.	
3. CNN Student News Guided Notes 1-5 *I can summarize events in a news story.	
4. Close Reading/Literacy Activity: Today we are_____ *I can complete a close reading or literacy strategy for something that I read. *I can organize and summarize information.	
Write your own goals for your school work for #s 5 and 6.	
5.	
6. *I can complete activities & lessons in my courses.	

Created by **Melissa Marini Švigelj-Smith** 2017-2019

7. Reflection sheet on goals today *I can reflect on my day and write honestly about whether or not I accomplished my short-term goals.	

In class today, my behavior goals are… Write your own personal goals for #s 3 & 4 *I can use strategies to maintain positive behaviors & reduce negative behaviors.	Did I …? Check if "yes"
1. I will keep a growth mindset.	
2. I will make healthy choices.	
3.	
4.	

DAILY REFLECTION

Explain what you did well today in at least one complete sentence. _____
_____

Explain how you would rate your performance in class today on a scale of 10 to 1, and explain why you ranked yourself that way. 10= I did my best   5= I tried half the time   1=I did not try at all
_____
_____

Write a complete sentence about one part of your work in class you would like to improve and explain why.
_____
_____

Choose to complete at least ONE of the writing prompts below. Circle which one you are completing.
1. I wish you would have known today that I…
2. I am really proud that today I…
3. My favorite part of today was…
4. I wonder if today I could...

_____
_____
_____

Created by **Melissa Marini Švigelj-Smith** 2017-2019

Name_____Date_____

Write one thing you are grateful (**thankful**) for today. Finding things to be thankful for helps improve our overall happiness. Happier people are more successful people._____

_____

Today, I am thankful learning is fun.

Remember to practice 4-7-8 breathing as needed, and to keep a growth mindset.

> **Develop a *GROWTH MINDSET* - *People who believe their talents can be developed (through hard work, good strategies & input from others) have a growth mindset. They tend to achieve more than those with a fixed mindset. ~Carol Dweck***

Instead of thinking...	Try thinking...
I give up	I won't stop until I succeed
I'm not good at this	How can I get better?
I can't be any better	I can always improve
This is too hard	This may take some time
I can't do this	I am going to learn to do this
My mistakes ruined me	I can learn from my mistakes
My plan didn't work	I can try another plan
I'm not smart	I can always learn new things
I'm jealous	I can learn from their success

4-7-8 Breathing
-Dr. Andrew Weil
Use this strategy to help you stay calm & to relax
4 - Breathe in as you count to 4
7 - Hold your breath as you count to 7
8 - Breathe out as you count to 8

[ESPN E60 Special Feature: Four Weeks in Ferguson](#) **(11 minutes)**

1. How did Ferguson, Missouri, become well known around the country?

   _____
   _____

2. Why was McCluer School closed?

   _____

3. What does Eugene think saved him when Darren Wilson made him pull over?

   _____

4. How does the player describe being on the football field?

   _____

CNN 10 STUDENT NEWS (10 minute show) *Write 5 things you learned from the news today.*

1. _____
   _____
   _____

2. _____
   _____
   _____

3. _____
   _____
   _____

4. _____
   _____
   _____

5. _____
   _____
   _____

Daily Goals Sheet   **I can statements for each day.*
This is the list of things that I want to accomplish (complete) today in class.

Tasks or assignments I need to complete in class **I can exercise strategies like deep breathing (4-7-8 breathing) to calm or focus myself.*	Completed? Check if "yes"
1. Entry journal prompt response & daily gratitude statement **I can recognize what I value and appreciate. *I can write a thoughtful & clear response to a writing prompt.*	
2. Daily Goals Sheet filled out **I can plan short-term goals in order to reach my long term goals.*	
3. CNN Student News Guided Notes 1-5 **I can summarize events in a news story.*	
4. Close Reading/Literacy Activity: Today we are_____ _____ **I can complete a close reading or literacy strategy for something that I read.* **I can organize and summarize information.*	
Write your own goals for your school work for #s 5 and 6.	
5.	
6. **I can complete activities & lessons in my courses.*	
7. Reflection sheet on goals today **I can reflect on my day and write honestly about whether or not I accomplished my short-term goals.*	

Created by **Melissa Marini Švigelj-Smith** 2017-2019

In class today, my behavior goals are… Write your own personal goals for #s 3 & 4 *I can use strategies to maintain positive behaviors & reduce negative behaviors.	Did I …? Check if "yes"
1. I will keep a growth mindset.	
2. I will make healthy choices.	
3.	
4.	

DAILY REFLECTION
Explain what you did well today in at least one complete sentence.
_____
_____

Explain how you would rate your performance in class today on a scale of 10 to 1, **and explain why** you ranked yourself that way. 10= I did my best 5= I tried half the time 1=I did not try at all
_____
_____

Write a complete sentence about one part of your work in class you would like to improve and explain why.
_____
_____

Choose to complete ONE of the writing prompts below. Circle which one you are completing.
1. I wish you would have known today that I…
2. I am really proud that today I…
3. My favorite part of today was…
4. I wonder if today I could...

_____
_____

Name_____ Date_____

Write one thing you are grateful (**thankful**) for today. Finding things to be thankful for helps improve our overall happiness. Happier people are more successful people._____
_____

Today, I am thankful class is so interesting.

Remember to practice 4-7-8 breathing as needed, and to keep a growth mindset.

> **Develop a *GROWTH MINDSET* -** *People who believe their talents can be developed (through hard work, good strategies & input from others) have a growth mindset. They tend to achieve more than those with a fixed mindset. Carol Dweck*

Instead of thinking...	Try thinking...
I give up	I won't stop until I succeed
I'm not good at this	How can I get better?
I can't be any better	I can always improve
This is too hard	This may take some time
I can't do this	I am going to learn to do this
My mistakes ruined me	I can learn from my mistakes
My plan didn't work	I can try another plan
I'm not smart	I can always learn new things
I'm jealous	I can learn from their success

4-7-8 Breathing
-Dr. Andrew Weil
Use this strategy to help you stay calm & to relax
4 - Breathe in as you count to 4
7 - Hold your breath as you count to 7
8 - Breathe out as you count to 8

[ESPN 30 for 30 - Ghosts of 'Ole Miss](#) **(50 minutes)**
Answer the questions as you watch the video.

1. Who was James Meredith?

2. Who are the sports teams "the rebels" named after?

3. Why are the federal marshals on campus in Mississippi?

4. Describe one thing that happens during the riots on campus.

5. How is James Meredith treated as he goes to class on campus?

6. What did the Ole Miss' coach tell the players before the homecoming game?

7. How did James Meredith react to the abuse he received on campus?

8. What did a cheerleader protest in 1982?

9. Name one other change on the Ole Miss campus in the past 30 years?

10. What might the saying "Even the darkest night has to give way to dawn" mean?

CNN 10 STUDENT NEWS (**10 minute show**) *Write 5 things you learned from the news today.*

1. _____
_____
_____

2. _____
_____
_____

3. _____
_____
_____

4. _____
_____
_____

5. _____
_____
_____

Daily Goals Sheet   *****I can statements for each day.**
This is the list of things that I want to accomplish (complete) today in class.

Tasks or assignments I need to complete in class *I can exercise strategies like deep breathing (4-7-8 breathing) to calm or focus myself.	Completed? Check if "yes"
1. Entry journal prompt response & daily gratitude statement *I can recognize what I value and appreciate. *I can write a thoughtful & clear response to a writing prompt.	
2. Daily Goals Sheet filled out *I can plan short-term goals in order to reach my long term goals.	
3. CNN Student News Guided Notes 1-5 *I can summarize events in a news story.	
4. Close Reading/Literacy Activity: Today we are_____ _____ *I can complete a close reading or literacy strategy for something that I read. *I can organize and summarize information.	
Write your own goals for your school work for #s 5 and 6.	
5.	

6. *I can complete activities & lessons in my courses.	
7. Reflection sheet on goals today *I can reflect on my day and write honestly about whether or not I accomplished my short-term goals.	

In class today, my behavior goals are… Write your own personal goals for #s 3 & 4 *I can use strategies to maintain positive behaviors & reduce negative behaviors.	Did I …? Check if "yes"
1. I will keep a growth mindset.	
2. I will make healthy choices.	
3.	
4.	

DAILY REFLECTION

Explain what you did well today in at least one complete sentence.
_____
_____

Explain how you would rate your performance in class today on a scale of 10 to 1, **and explain why** you ranked yourself that way. 10= I did my best 5= I tried half the time 1=I did not try at all
_____
_____

Write a complete sentence about one part of your work in class you would like to improve and explain why.
_____
_____

Choose to complete ONE of the writing prompts below. Circle which one you are completing.
1. I wish you would have known today that I…
2. I am really proud that today I…
3. My favorite part of today was…
4. I wonder if today I could...

_____
_____

Created by **Melissa Marini Švigelj-Smith** 2017-2019

Name_____ Date_____

Write one thing you are grateful **(thankful)** for today. Finding things to be thankful for helps improve our overall happiness. Happier people are more successful people._____

_____

Today, I am thankful for a chance to learn from others.

Remember to practice 4-7-8 breathing as needed, and to keep a growth mindset.

Develop a *GROWTH MINDSET* - *People who believe their talents can be developed (through hard work, good strategies & input from others) have a growth mindset. They tend to achieve more than those with a fixed mindset. ~Carol Dweck*

Instead of thinking...	Try thinking...
I give up	I won't stop until I succeed
I'm not good at this	How can I get better?
I can't be any better	I can always improve
This is too hard	This may take some time
I can't do this	I am going to learn to do this
My mistakes ruined me	I can learn from my mistakes
My plan didn't work	I can try another plan
I'm not smart	I can always learn new things
I'm jealous	I can learn from their success

4-7-8 Breathing
-Dr. Andrew Weil
Use this strategy to help you stay calm & to relax
4 - Breathe in as you count to 4
7 - Hold your breath as you count to 7
8 - Breathe out as you count to 8

E60: Chris Singleton "Love is Stronger" (Charleston, SC) (30 minutes)

5. Why is Charleston called "The Holy City?"

_____

6. How far away from his home was the school that Chris chose to go to?

_____

7. How does Chris exhibit a "growth mindset" or positive work habits?

_____

8. Write something positive you learned about Chris' mother.

_____

9. How was stepping onto the field after the nine murders different for Chris?

_____

Created by **Melissa Marini Švigelj-Smith** 2017-2019

CNN 10 STUDENT NEWS (10 minute show) *Write 5 things you learned from the news today.*

1. _____
   _____
   _____
2. _____
   _____
   _____
3. _____
   _____
   _____
4. _____
   _____
   _____
5. _____
   _____
   _____

Daily Goals Sheet *I can statements for each day.*
This is the list of things that I want to accomplish (complete) today in class.

Tasks or assignments I need to complete in class *I can exercise strategies like deep breathing (4-7-8 breathing) to calm or focus myself.	Completed? Check if "yes"
1. Entry journal prompt response & daily gratitude statement *I can recognize what I value and appreciate. *I can write a thoughtful & clear response to a writing prompt.	
2. Daily Goals Sheet filled out *I can plan short-term goals in order to reach my long term goals.	
3. CNN Student News Guided Notes 1-5 *I can summarize events in a news story.	
4. Close Reading/Literacy Activity: Today we are_____ _____ *I can complete a close reading or literacy strategy for something that I read. *I can organize and summarize information.	
Write your own goals for your school work for #s 5 and 6.	
5.	
6. *I can complete activities & lessons in my courses.	
7. Reflection sheet on goals today	

Created by **Melissa Marini Švigelj-Smith** 2017-2019

	Did I...? Check if "yes"
*I can reflect on my day and write honestly about whether or not I accomplished my short-term goals.	

In class today, my behavior goals are… Write your own personal goals for #s 3 & 4 *I can use strategies to maintain positive behaviors & reduce negative behaviors.	Did I ...? Check if "yes"
1. I will keep a growth mindset.	
2. I will make healthy choices.	
3.	
4.	

DAILY REFLECTION

Explain what you did well today in at least one complete sentence.
_____
_____

Explain how you would rate your performance in class today on a scale of 10 to 1, **and explain why** you ranked yourself that way. 10= I did my best 5= I tried half the time 1=I did not try at all
_____
_____

Write a complete sentence about one part of your work in class you would like to improve and explain why.
_____
_____
_____

Choose to complete ONE of the writing prompts below. Circle which one you are completing.
1. I wish you would have known today that I…
2. I am really proud that today I…
3. My favorite part of today was…
4. I wonder if today I could...

_____
_____

Name_____ Date_____

Write one thing you are grateful (**thankful**) for today. Finding things to be thankful for helps improve our overall happiness. Happier people are more successful people._____
_____
_____

Today, I am thankful our world is so interesting!

Remember to practice 4-7-8 breathing as needed and to keep a growth mindset.

Develop a GROWTH MINDSET - People who believe their talents can be developed (through hard work, good strategies & input from others) have a growth mindset. They tend to achieve more than those with a fixed mindset. ~Dr. Carol Dweck

🚫 Instead of thinking...	🌳 Try thinking...
I give up	I won't stop until I succeed
I'm not good at this	How can I get better?
I can't be any better	I can always improve
This is too hard	This may take some time
I can't do this	I am going to learn to do this
My mistakes ruined me	I can learn from my mistakes
My plan didn't work	I can try another plan
I'm not smart	I can always learn new things
I'm jealous	I can learn from their success

4-7-8 Breathing
Use this strategy to help you stay calm & to relax
4 - Breathe in as you count to 4
7 - Hold your breath as you count to 7
8 - Breathe out as you count to 8

~Dr. Andrew Weil

[Facing Fear - Sean Wilson (5 mins)](#)

1. Why did Mr. Wilson's dream "die" after he saw the movie "Deep Blue Sea?"

2. Name something that created fear in Mr. Wilson as a young man?

3. What did Mr. Wilson say he did at age 16 that left his family and community as collateral damage?

4. What Is something that Mr. Wilson accomplished that he never thought he was capable of doing?

5. What does Mr. Wilson say "trumps fear every time?"

CNN 10 STUDENT NEWS **(10 minute show)** *Write 5 things you learned from the news today.*

1._____

2._____

3._____

4._____

5._____

Daily Goals Sheet *I can statements for each day.
This is the list of things that I want to accomplish (complete) today in class.

Tasks or assignments I need to complete in class *I can exercise strategies like deep breathing (4-7-8 breathing) to calm or focus myself.	Completed? Check if "yes"
1. Entry journal prompt response & daily gratitude statement *I can recognize what I value and appreciate. *I can write a thoughtful & clear response to a writing prompt.	
2. Daily Goals Sheet filled out *I can plan short-term goals in order to reach my long term goals.	
3. CNN Student News Guided Notes 1-5 *I can summarize events in a news story.	
4. Close Reading/Literacy Activity: Today we are_____ _____ *I can complete a close reading or literacy strategy for something that I read. *I can organize and summarize information.	
Write your own goals for your school work for #s 5 and 6.	
5.	
6. *I can complete activities & lessons in my courses.	
7. Reflection sheet on goals today *I can reflect on my day and write honestly about whether or not I	

Created by **Melissa Marini Švigelj-Smith** 2017-2019

| accomplished my short-term goals. | |

In class today, my behavior goals are… **Write your own personal goals for #s 3 & 4** *I can use strategies to maintain positive behaviors & reduce negative behaviors.	Did I …? Check if "yes"
1. I will keep a growth mindset.	
2. I will make healthy choices.	
3.	
4.	

DAILY REFLECTION
Explain what you did well today in at least one complete sentence.
_____
_____

Explain how you would rate your performance in class today on a scale of 10 to 1, and explain why you ranked yourself that way. 10= I did my best 5= I tried half the time 1=I did not try at all
_____
_____
_____

Write a complete sentence about one part of your work in class you would like to improve and explain why.
_____
_____
_____

Choose to complete at least ONE of the writing prompts below. Circle which one you are completing.
1. I wish you would have known today that I…
2. I am really proud that today I…
3. My favorite part of today was…
4. I wonder if today I could...
_____
_____
_____

Name_____ Date_____

Write one thing you are grateful (**thankful**) for today. Finding things to be thankful for helps improve our overall happiness. Happier people are more successful people._____

_____

Today, I am thankful for the wisdom of others.
[4 Thoughts About Gratitude That Could Change Your Life | Digital Original | Oprah Winfrey Network](#) **(2.5 minutes)**
List possible benefits being grateful may bring or reasons being grateful is important according to the video clips, (at least four).

1._____
_____
2._____
_____
3._____
_____
4._____
_____

Remember to practice 4-7-8 breathing as needed, and to keep a growth mindset.

> **Develop a *GROWTH MINDSET* -** People who believe their talents can be developed (through hard work, good strategies & input from others) have a growth mindset. They tend to achieve more than those with a fixed mindset. ~Dr. Carol Dweck

Instead of thinking...	Try thinking...
I give up	I won't stop until I succeed
I'm not good at this	How can I get better?
I can't be any better	I can always improve
This is too hard	This may take some time
I can't do this	I am going to learn to do this
My mistakes ruined me	I can learn from my mistakes
My plan didn't work	I can try another plan
I'm not smart	I can always learn new things
I'm jealous	I can learn from their success

4-7-8 Breathing
Use this strategy to help you stay calm & to relax
4 - Breathe in as you count to 4
7 - Hold your breath as you count to 7
8 - Breathe out as you count to 8

~Dr. Andrew Weil

[Breathing Space: Solitude on the Pacific Crest Trail | SuperSoul Sunday | Oprah Winfrey Network](#) **(1.5 minutes)**

Use this breathing space video to practice 4-7-8 breathing. Write what to do for each stage when practicing the 4-7-8 breathing method, and answer the question before you begin.

1. 4-
2. 7-
3. 8-
4. & 5. List two benefits of practicing 4-7-8 breathing.
   _____
   _____

[CNN 10 STUDENT NEWS](#) **(10 minute show)** *Write **5** things you learned from the news today.*

1. _____
2. _____
3. _____
4. _____
5. _____

Daily Goals Sheet   **I can statements for each day.*
This is the list of things that I want to accomplish (complete) today in class.

Tasks or assignments I need to complete in class	Completed? Check if "yes"
*I can exercise strategies like deep breathing (4-7-8 breathing) to calm or focus myself.	
1. Entry journal prompt response & daily gratitude statement *I can recognize what I value and appreciate. *I can write a thoughtful & clear response to a writing prompt.	
2. Daily Goals Sheet filled out *I can plan short-term goals in order to reach my long term goals.	
3. CNN Student News Guided Notes 1-5 *I can summarize events in a news story.	
4. Close Reading/Literacy Activity: Today we are_____ *I can complete a close reading or literacy strategy for something that I	

Created by **Melissa Marini Švigelj-Smith** 2017-2019

read. *I can organize and summarize information.	
Write your own goals for your school work for #s 5 and 6.	
5.	
6. *I can complete activities & lessons in my online courses.	
7. Reflection sheet on goals today *I can reflect on my day and write honestly about whether or not I accomplished my short-term goals.	

In class today, my behavior goals are… **Write your own personal goals for #s 3 & 4** *I can use strategies to maintain positive behaviors & reduce negative behaviors.	Did I …? Check if "yes"
1. I will keep a growth mindset.	
2. I will make healthy choices.	
3.	
4.	

DAILY REFLECTION

Explain what you did well today in at least one complete sentence. _____
_____

Explain how you would rate your performance in class today on a scale of 10 to 1, and explain why you ranked yourself that way. 10= I did my best 5= I tried half the time 1=I did not try at all
_____
_____

Write a complete sentence about one part of your work in class you would like to improve and explain why.
_____
_____

Choose to complete at least ONE of the writing prompts below. Circle which one you are completing.
1. I wish you would have known today that I…
2. I am really proud that today I…
3. My favorite part of today was…
4. I wonder if today I could...

_____
_____

Name_____ Date_____

Write one thing you are grateful **(thankful)** for today. Finding things to be thankful for helps improve our overall happiness. Happier people are more successful people._____

_____

Today, I am thankful for healthy competitions.
Remember to practice 4-7-8 breathing as needed, and to keep a growth mindset.

> **Develop a *GROWTH MINDSET* -** People who believe their talents can be developed (through hard work, good strategies & input from others) have a growth mindset. They tend to achieve more than those with a fixed mindset. ~Dr. Carol Dweck

Instead of thinking...	Try thinking...
I give up	I won't stop until I succeed
I'm not good at this	How can I get better?
I can't be any better	I can always improve
This is too hard	This may take some time
I can't do this	I am going to learn to do this
My mistakes ruined me	I can learn from my mistakes
My plan didn't work	I can try another plan
I'm not smart	I can always learn new things
I'm jealous	I can learn from their success

4-7-8 Breathing
Use this strategy to help you stay calm & to relax
4 - Breathe in as you count to 4
7 - Hold your breath as you count to 7
8 - Breathe out as you count to 8

~Dr. Andrew Weil

[Fox Sports Tour of Negro League Baseball Museum](#)

(6 minutes)

1. Why did the museum curators want visitors to look through a fence at the *Field of Legends* when they arrive to the museum?

2. 3. 4. *Write one fact about each of the following:*

Name	Fact
2. Rube Foster	
3. Hank Aaron	

4. Jackie Robinson	

CNN 10 STUDENT NEWS (**10 minute show**) *Write **5** things you learned from the news today.*

1._____

2._____

3._____

4._____

5._____

Daily Goals Sheet   *****I can statements for each day.**
This is the list of things that I want to accomplish (complete) today in class.

Tasks or assignments I need to complete in class *I can exercise strategies like deep breathing (4-7-8 breathing) to calm or focus myself.	Completed? Check if "yes"
1. Entry journal prompt response & daily gratitude statement *I can recognize what I value and appreciate. *I can write a thoughtful & clear response to a writing prompt.	
2. Daily Goals Sheet filled out *I can plan short-term goals in order to reach my long term goals.	
3. CNN Student News Guided Notes 1-5 *I can summarize events in a news story.	
4. Close Reading/Literacy Activity: Today we are_____ _____ *I can complete a close reading or literacy strategy for something that I read. *I can organize and summarize information.	
Write your own goals for your school work for #s 5 and 6.	
5.	
6. *I can complete activities & lessons in my courses.	
7. Reflection sheet on goals today *I can reflect on my day and write honestly about whether or not I	

Created by **Melissa Marini Švigelj-Smith** 2017-2019

| accomplished my short-term goals. | |

In class today, my behavior goals are… **Write your own personal goals for #s 3 & 4** *I can use strategies to maintain positive behaviors & reduce negative behaviors.	**Did I …?** **Check if** **"yes"**
1. I will keep a growth mindset.	
2. I will make healthy choices.	
3.	
4.	

DAILY REFLECTION
Explain what you did well today in at least one complete sentence.
___
___

Explain how you would rate your performance in class today on a scale of 10 to 1, **and explain why** you ranked yourself that way. 10= I did my best 5= I tried half the time 1=I did not try at all
___
___

Write a complete sentence about one part of your work in class you would like to improve and explain why.
___
___
___

Choose to complete at least ONE of the writing prompts below. Circle which one you are completing.
1. I wish you would have known today that I…
2. I am really proud that today I…
3. My favorite part of today was…
4. I wonder if today I could...

___
___

Name_____Date_____

Write one thing you are grateful (**thankful**) for today. Finding things to be thankful for helps improve our overall happiness. Happier people are more successful people._____

_____

Today I am thankful for being able to go to school.
Remember to practice 4-7-8 breathing as needed, and to keep a growth mindset.

Develop a *GROWTH MINDSET* - People who believe their talents can be developed (through hard work, good strategies & input from others) have a growth mindset. They tend to achieve more than those with a fixed mindset. ~Dr. Carol Dweck

🚫 Instead of thinking...	🌳 Try thinking...
I give up	I won't stop until I succeed
I'm not good at this	How can I get better?
I can't be any better	I can always improve
This is too hard	This may take some time
I can't do this	I am going to learn to do this
My mistakes ruined me	I can learn from my mistakes
My plan didn't work	I can try another plan
I'm not smart	I can always learn new things
I'm jealous	I can learn from their success

Freeman Hrabowski: 4 pillars of college success in science (& in school)
(15 minute TED Talk)

1. Which state did Freeman grow up in?

2. Which year did Freeman go to jail with Dr. Martin Luther King?

3. 4. 5. 6. What are the 4 Pillars of Success that Freeman found to be important at the University of Baltimore, Maryland?

    a.

    b.

    c.

d.

7. Fill in the blank for this sentence from Aristotle that Freeman quotes:

   _____ *not chance determines your destiny.*

8. What do **you think** students need to be successful in school?

   _____

   _____

CNN 10 STUDENT NEWS (10 minute show) *Write 5 things you learned from the news today.*

1. _____
   _____

2. _____
   _____

3. _____
   _____

4. _____
   _____

5. _____
   _____

Daily Goals Sheet   *****I can statements for each day.**
This is the list of things that I want to accomplish (complete) today in class.

Tasks or assignments I need to complete in class	Completed? Check if "yes"
*I can exercise strategies like deep breathing (4-7-8 breathing) to calm or focus myself.	
1. Entry journal prompt response & daily gratitude statement *I can recognize what I value and appreciate. *I can write a thoughtful & clear response to a writing prompt.	
2. Daily Goals Sheet filled out *I can plan short-term goals in order to reach my long term goals.	
3. CNN Student News Guided Notes 1-5 *I can summarize events in a news story.	
4. Close Reading/Literacy Activity: Today we are_____ _____ *I can complete a close reading or literacy strategy for something that I read. *I can organize and summarize information.	

Created by **Melissa Marini Švigelj-Smith** 2017-2019

Write your own goals for your school work for #s 5 and 6.	
5.	
6. *I can complete activities & lessons in my online courses.	
7. Reflection sheet on goals today *I can reflect on my day and write honestly about whether or not I accomplished my short-term goals.	

In class today, my behavior goals are… Write your own personal goals for #s 3 & 4 *I can use strategies to maintain positive behaviors & reduce negative behaviors.	Did I …? Check if "yes"
1. I will keep a growth mindset.	
2. I will make healthy choices.	
3.	
4.	

DAILY REFLECTION

Explain what you did well today in at least one complete sentence. _____
_____

Explain how you would rate your performance in class today on a scale of 10 to 1, and explain why you ranked yourself that way. 10= I did my best 5= I tried half the time 1=I did not try at all
_____
_____

Write a complete sentence about one part of your work in class that you would like to improve and explain why.
_____
_____

Choose to complete at least ONE of the writing prompts below. Circle which one you are completing.
1. I wish that you would have known today that I…
2. I am really proud that today I…
3. My favorite part of today was…
4. I wonder if today I could...

_____
_____

Created by **Melissa Marini Švigelj-Smith** 2017-2019

Name_____ Date_____

Write one thing you are grateful (**thankful**) for today. Finding things to be thankful for helps improve our overall happiness. Happier people are more successful people._____
_____
_____

Today, I am thankful for creative minds!

Remember to practice 4-7-8 breathing as needed, and to keep a growth mindset.

Develop a GROWTH MINDSET - People who believe their talents can be developed (through hard work, good strategies & input from others) have a growth mindset. They tend to achieve more than those with a fixed mindset. ~Dr. Carol Dweck

Instead of thinking...	Try thinking...
I give up	I won't stop until I succeed
I'm not good at this	How can I get better?
I can't be any better	I can always improve
This is too hard	This may take some time
I can't do this	I am going to learn to do this
My mistakes ruined me	I can learn from my mistakes
My plan didn't work	I can try another plan
I'm not smart	I can always learn new things
I'm jealous	I can learn from their success

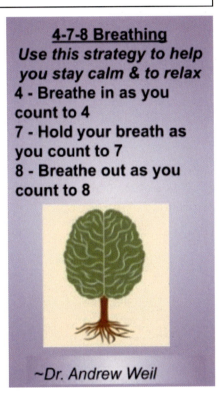

Friends (spoken word) by Suli Breaks **(3 minutes)**
A few lines from the poem:

They say if you truly want to know yourself
Look at your five closest friends.
Because your reflection of the people you spend most of your time with
Whether you like it or not, like them or not, friends can do two things:
Either push us forward or pull us back...

Before the Poem:

1. **Predict** what you think his poem will be about._____
_____

After you listen to the poem:
2. **Paraphrase** (put in your own words) what this poem was about. _____

Created by **Melissa Marini Švigelj-Smith** 2017-2019

3. Describe the **Conflict** or problems that are discussed in this poem. _____

4. Write any **Literary Devices** that were used in the poem (metaphor, simile, rhyming) _____

5. What is the **Tone** (mood) of the poem? (happy, sad, angry, suspenseful) _____

6. Use words or lines from the poem to support your answer for question 6. Use **evidence** from the text that shows the tone. _____

7. What is the **Theme** of the poem? _____

8. What words or lines (**evidence** from the text) in the poem helped you recognize and understand the theme? _____

CNN 10 STUDENT NEWS **(10 minute show)** *Write 5 things you learned from the news today.*

1. _____

2. _____

3. _____

4. _____

5. _____

Created by **Melissa Marini Švigelj-Smith** 2017-2019

Daily Goals Sheet *I can statements for each day.
This is the list of things that I want to accomplish (complete) today in class.

Tasks or assignments I need to complete in class *I can exercise strategies like deep breathing (4-7-8 breathing) to calm or focus myself.	Completed? Check if "yes"
1. Entry journal prompt response & daily gratitude statement *I can recognize what I value and appreciate. *I can write a thoughtful & clear response to a writing prompt.	
2. Daily Goals Sheet filled out *I can plan short-term goals in order to reach my long term goals.	
3. CNN Student News Guided Notes 1-5 *I can summarize events in a news story.	
4. Close Reading/Literacy Activity: Today we are_____ *I can complete a close reading or literacy strategy for something that I read. *I can organize and summarize information.	
Write your own goals for your school work for #s 5 and 6.	
5.	
6. *I can complete activities & lessons in my courses.	
7. Reflection sheet on goals today *I can reflect on my day and write honestly about whether or not I accomplished my short-term goals.	

In class today, my behavior goals are… Write your own personal goals for #s 3 & 4 *I can use strategies to maintain positive behaviors & reduce negative behaviors.	Did I …? Check if "yes"
1. I will keep a growth mindset.	
2. I will make healthy choices.	
3.	
4.	

Created by **Melissa Marini Švigelj-Smith** 2017-2019

DAILY REFLECTION

Explain what you did well today in at least one complete sentence.
_____
_____

Explain how you would rate your performance in class today on a scale of 10 to 1, and explain why you ranked yourself that way. 10= I did my best 5= I tried half the time 1=I did not try at all
_____
_____
_____

Write a complete sentence about one part of your work in class you would like to improve and explain why.
_____
_____
_____

Choose to complete at least ONE of the writing prompts below. Circle which one you are completing.
1. I wish you would have known today that I…
2. I am really proud that today I…
3. My favorite part of today was…
4. I wonder if today I could...

_____
_____
_____

Name_____Date_____

Write one thing you are grateful (**thankful**) for today. Finding things to be thankful for helps improve our overall happiness. Happier people are more successful people._____
_____

Today I am thankful for teeth.
Remember to practice 4-7-8 breathing as needed, and to keep a growth mindset.

> **Develop a *GROWTH MINDSET*** - *People who believe their talents can be developed (through hard work, good strategies & input from others) have a growth mindset. They tend to achieve more than those with a fixed mindset. ~Dr. Carol Dweck*

Instead of thinking...	Try thinking...
I give up	I won't stop until I succeed
I'm not good at this	How can I get better?
I can't be any better	I can always improve
This is too hard	This may take some time
I can't do this	I am going to learn to do this
My mistakes ruined me	I can learn from my mistakes
My plan didn't work	I can try another plan
I'm not smart	I can always learn new things
I'm jealous	I can learn from their success

TEDxTalk - Grateful for the Opportunity, M. Clark (5 minutes)

1. What are FOUR things that Mr. Clark is appreciative of or grateful for?
    A.
    B.
    C.
    D.
5. What is M. Clark's call to action?

CNN 10 STUDENT NEWS **(10 minute show)** *Write 5 things you learned from the news today.*

1. _____
   _____
   _____
2. _____
   _____
   _____
3. _____
   _____
   _____
4. _____
   _____
   _____
5. _____
   _____
   _____

Daily Goals Sheet   **I can statements for each day.*
This is the list of things that I want to accomplish (complete) today in class.

Tasks or assignments I need to complete in class *I can exercise strategies like deep breathing (4-7-8 breathing) to calm or focus myself.	Completed? Check if "yes"
1. Entry journal prompt response & daily gratitude statement *I can recognize what I value and appreciate. *I can write a thoughtful & clear response to a writing prompt.	
2. Daily Goals Sheet filled out *I can plan short-term goals in order to reach my long term goals.	
3. CNN Student News Guided Notes 1-5 *I can summarize events in a news story.	
4. Close Reading/Literacy Activity: Today we are_____ _____ *I can complete a close reading or literacy strategy for something that I read. *I can organize and summarize information.	
Write your own goals for your school work for #s 5 and 6.	
5.	
6. *I can complete activities & lessons in my courses.	
7. Reflection sheet on goals today *I can reflect on my day and write honestly about whether or not I	

Created by **Melissa Marini Švigelj-Smith** 2017-2019

| accomplished my short-term goals. | |

In class today, my behavior goals are… Write your own personal goals for #s 3 & 4 *I can use strategies to maintain positive behaviors & reduce negative behaviors.	Did I …? Check if "yes"
1. I will keep a growth mindset.	
2. I will make healthy choices.	
3.	
4.	

DAILY REFLECTION

Explain what you did well today in at least one complete sentence. _____
_____

Explain how you would rate your performance in class today on a scale of 10 to 1, and explain why you ranked yourself that way. 10= I did my best 5= I tried half the time 1=I did not try at all
_____
_____

Write a complete sentence about one part of your work in class you would like to improve and explain why.
_____
_____

Choose to complete at least ONE of the writing prompts below. Circle which one you are completing.
1. I wish you would have known today that I…
2. I am really proud that today I…
3. My favorite part of today was…
4. I wonder if today I could...
_____
_____
_____

Name_____ Date_____

Write one thing you are grateful (**thankful**) for today. Finding things to be thankful for helps improve our overall happiness. Happier people are more successful people._____
_____

Today I am thankful for the creativity of others.

Remember to practice 4-7-8 breathing as needed, and to keep a growth mindset.

> **Develop a *GROWTH MINDSET* -** People who believe their talents can be developed *(through hard work, good strategies & input from others)* have a growth mindset. They tend to achieve more than those with a fixed mindset. *~Dr. Carol Dweck*

Instead of thinking...	Try thinking...
I give up	I won't stop until I succeed
I'm not good at this	How can I get better?
I can't be any better	I can always improve
This is too hard	This may take some time
I can't do this	I am going to learn to do this
My mistakes ruined me	I can learn from my mistakes
My plan didn't work	I can try another plan
I'm not smart	I can always learn new things
I'm jealous	I can learn from their success

4-7-8 Breathing
Use this strategy to help you stay calm & to relax
4 - Breathe in as you count to 4
7 - Hold your breath as you count to 7
8 - Breathe out as you count to 8

~Dr. Andrew Weil

[Heroes & Villains: Is Hip Hop a Cancer or a Cure?](#) **Lecrae (18 minute TED Talk)**

1. Simply put, in literature a protagonist is a _____ and an antagonist is a _____.

2. Where did the word "villain" come from?

3. What is one criticism of hip hop from conservative talkers?

4. What was hip hop like in the beginning?

5. Name something that was going on in the 1980s.

6. Name something that was going on in the 1990s.

7. How did hip hop respond to events that happened in the 1980s and 1990s?

8. How can hip hop stop being a perpetrator of villainous activity?

9. What does Lecrae say that every story has?

CNN 10 STUDENT NEWS **(10 minute show)** *Write **5** things you learned from the news today.*

1. _____
   _____
   _____
2. _____
   _____
   _____
3. _____
   _____
   _____
4. _____
   _____
   _____
5. _____
   _____
   _____

Daily Goals Sheet   ***I can statements for each day.**
This is the list of things that I want to accomplish (complete) today in class.

Tasks or assignments I need to complete in class *I can exercise strategies like deep breathing (4-7-8 breathing) to calm or focus myself.	Completed? Check if "yes"
1. Entry journal prompt response & daily gratitude statement *I can recognize what I value and appreciate. *I can write a thoughtful & clear response to a writing prompt.	
2. Daily Goals Sheet filled out *I can plan short-term goals in order to reach my long term goals.	
3. CNN Student News Guided Notes 1-5 *I can summarize events in a news story.	
4. Close Reading/Literacy Activity: Today we are_____ _____ *I can complete a close reading or literacy strategy for something that I read. *I can organize and summarize information.	
Write your own goals for your school work for #s 5 and 6.	
5.	
6.	

Created by **Melissa Marini Švigelj-Smith** 2017-2019

*I can complete activities & lessons in my courses.	
7. Reflection sheet on goals today *I can reflect on my day and write honestly about whether or not I accomplished my short-term goals.	

In class today, my behavior goals are… Write your own personal goals for #s 3 & 4 *I can use strategies to maintain positive behaviors & reduce negative behaviors.	Did I …? Check if "yes"
1. I will keep a growth mindset.	
2. I will make healthy choices.	
3.	
4.	

DAILY REFLECTION

Explain what you did well today in at least one complete sentence. _____
_____

Explain how you would rate your performance in class today on a scale of 10 to 1, and explain why you ranked yourself that way. 10= I did my best 5= I tried half the time 1=I did not try at all
_____
_____

Write a complete sentence about one part of your work in class you would like to improve and explain why.
_____
_____

Choose to complete at least ONE of the writing prompts below. Circle which one you are completing.
1. I wish you would have known today that I…
2. I am really proud that today I…
3. My favorite part of today was…
4. I wonder if today I could...

_____
_____
_____

Created by **Melissa Marini Švigelj-Smith** 2017-2019

Name_____Date_____

Write one thing you are grateful (**thankful**) for today. Finding things to be thankful for helps improve our overall happiness. Happier people are more successful people._____
_____

Today I am thankful for great plays to read and watch.
Remember to practice 4-7-8 breathing as needed, and to keep a growth mindset.

> **Develop a *GROWTH MINDSET* -** *People who believe their talents can be developed (through hard work, good strategies & input from others) have a growth mindset. They tend to achieve more than those with a fixed mindset. ~Dr. Carol Dweck*

Instead of thinking...	Try thinking...
I give up	I won't stop until I succeed
I'm not good at this	How can I get better?
I can't be any better	I can always improve
This is too hard	This may take some time
I can't do this	I am going to learn to do this
My mistakes ruined me	I can learn from my mistakes
My plan didn't work	I can try another plan
I'm not smart	I can always learn new things
I'm jealous	I can learn from their success

4-7-8 Breathing
Use this strategy to help you stay calm & to relax
4 - Breathe in as you count to 4
7 - Hold your breath as you count to 7
8 - Breathe out as you count to 8

~Dr. Andrew Weil

[Hip Hop & Shakespeare? Akala at TEDxAldeburgh](#) **(20 minutes)**

1. Name a hip hop artist that Akala quoted during his introduction.

2. What does iambic pentameter allow artists to do?

3. What does music imitate?

4. What does Hip Hop literally mean?

5. What is the 5th element of Hip Hop?

6. What kind of question does Akala think we should be asking about education?

7. Name one character from Shakespeare that Akala mentions.

Created by **Melissa Marini Švigelj-Smith** 2017-2019

CNN 10 STUDENT NEWS (10 minute show) *Write 5 things you learned from the news today.*

1. _____
   _____
   _____
2. _____
   _____
   _____
3. _____
   _____
   _____
4. _____
   _____
   _____
5. _____
   _____
   _____

Daily Goals Sheet   **I can statements for each day.*
This is the list of things that I want to accomplish (complete) today in class.

Tasks or assignments I need to complete in class *I can exercise strategies like deep breathing (4-7-8 breathing) to calm or focus myself.	Completed? Check if "yes"
1. Entry journal prompt response & daily gratitude statement *I can recognize what I value and appreciate. *I can write a thoughtful & clear response to a writing prompt.	
2. Daily Goals Sheet filled out *I can plan short-term goals in order to reach my long term goals.	
3. CNN Student News Guided Notes 1-5 *I can summarize events in a news story.	
4. Close Reading/Literacy Activity: Today we are_____ _____ *I can complete a close reading or literacy strategy for something that I read. *I can organize and summarize information.	
Write your own goals for your school work for #s 5 and 6.	
5.	
6. *I can complete activities & lessons in my courses.	
7. Reflection sheet on goals today *I can reflect on my day and write honestly about whether or not I	

| accomplished my short-term goals. | |

In class today, my behavior goals are… Write your own personal goals for #s 3 & 4 *I can use strategies to maintain positive behaviors & reduce negative behaviors.	Did I …? Check if "yes"
1. I will keep a growth mindset.	
2. I will make healthy choices.	
3.	
4.	

DAILY REFLECTION

Explain what you did well today in at least one complete sentence. _____
_____

Explain how you would rate your performance in class today on a scale of 10 to 1, and explain why you ranked yourself that way. 10= I did my best 5= I tried half the time 1=I did not try at all
_____
_____

Write a complete sentence about one part of your work in class you would like to improve and explain why.
_____
_____

Choose to complete at least ONE of the writing prompts below. Circle which one you are completing.
1. I wish you would have known today that I…
2. I am really proud that today I…
3. My favorite part of today was…
4. I wonder if today I could...

_____
_____
_____

Created by **Melissa Marini Švigelj-Smith** 2017-2019

Name_____ Date_____

Write one thing you are grateful **(thankful)** for today. Finding things to be thankful for helps improve our overall happiness. Happier people are more successful people._____
_____

Today I am thankful for people working for justice.
Remember to practice 4-7-8 breathing as needed, and to keep a growth mindset.

> **Develop a GROWTH MINDSET -** *People who believe their talents can be developed (through hard work, good strategies & input from others) have a growth mindset. They tend to achieve more than those with a fixed mindset. ~Dr. Carol Dweck*

Instead of thinking...	Try thinking...
I give up	I won't stop until I succeed
I'm not good at this	How can I get better?
I can't be any better	I can always improve
This is too hard	This may take some time
I can't do this	I am going to learn to do this
My mistakes ruined me	I can learn from my mistakes
My plan didn't work	I can try another plan
I'm not smart	I can always learn new things
I'm jealous	I can learn from their success

4-7-8 Breathing
Use this strategy to help you stay calm & to relax
4 - Breathe in as you count to 4
7 - Hold your breath as you count to 7
8 - Breathe out as you count to 8

~Dr. Andrew Weil

[How I Help Free Innocent People from Prison: Ronald Sullivan](#) *(12 minutes) TEDx Talk*
Answer the questions as you watch the video.

1. Where was Jonathan Fleming when the murder he was accused of occurred?

2. How did Jonathan Fleming prove that he was innocent?

3. How many people were released after a year of reviewing prosecutor's cases?

4. Where was one of the eyewitnesses actually at when she claimed to have witnessed a crime?

5. Why couldn't Mr. Stuckey leave prison after he was found innocent?

6. How can everyone take a minute for justice each day?

Created by **Melissa Marini Švigelj-Smith** 2017-2019

7. What does Professor Sullivan say justice is?

CNN 10 STUDENT NEWS (10 minute show)
Write 5 things you learned from the news today.

1. _____
2. _____
3. _____
4. _____
5. _____

Daily Goals Sheet   *I can statements for each day.

This is the list of things that I want to accomplish (complete) today in class.

Tasks or assignments I need to complete in class *I can exercise strategies like deep breathing (4-7-8 breathing) to calm or focus myself.	Completed? Check if "yes"
1. Entry journal prompt response & daily gratitude statement *I can recognize what I value and appreciate. *I can write a thoughtful & clear response to a writing prompt.	
2. Daily Goals Sheet filled out *I can plan short-term goals in order to reach my long term goals.	
3. CNN Student News Guided Notes 1-5 *I can summarize events in a news story.	
4. Close Reading/Literacy Activity: Today we are _____ *I can complete a close reading or literacy strategy for something that I read. *I can organize and summarize information.	
Write your own goals for your school work for #s 5 and 6.	
5.	
6.	

*I can complete activities & lessons in my courses.	
7. Reflection sheet on goals today *I can reflect on my day and write honestly about whether or not I accomplished my short-term goals.	

In class today, my behavior goals are… Write your own personal goals for #s 3 & 4 *I can use strategies to maintain positive behaviors & reduce negative behaviors.	Did I …? Check if "yes"
1. I will keep a growth mindset.	
2. I will make healthy choices.	
3.	
4.	

DAILY REFLECTION

Explain what you did well today in at least one complete sentence. _____
_____

Explain how you would rate your performance in class today on a scale of 10 to 1, and explain why you ranked yourself that way. 10= I did my best 5= I tried half the time 1=I did not try at all
_____
_____

Write a complete sentence about one part of your work in class you would like to improve and explain why.
_____
_____

Choose to complete at least ONE of the writing prompts below. Circle which one you are completing.
1. I wish you would have known today that I…
2. I am really proud that today I…
3. My favorite part of today was…
4. I wonder if today I could...

_____
_____
_____

Name_____Date_____

Write one thing you are grateful (**thankful**) for today. Finding things to be thankful for helps improve our overall happiness. Happier people are more successful people._____

_____

Today I am thankful for warm breezes.
Remember to practice 4-7-8 breathing as needed, and to keep a growth mindset.

> **Develop a *GROWTH MINDSET* -** People who believe their talents can be developed (through hard work, good strategies & input from others) have a growth mindset. They tend to achieve more than those with a fixed mindset. ~Dr. Carol Dweck

Instead of thinking...	Try thinking...
I give up	I won't stop until I succeed
I'm not good at this	How can I get better?
I can't be any better	I can always improve
This is too hard	This may take some time
I can't do this	I am going to learn to do this
My mistakes ruined me	I can learn from my mistakes
My plan didn't work	I can try another plan
I'm not smart	I can always learn new things
I'm jealous	I can learn from their success

4-7-8 Breathing
Use this strategy to help you stay calm & to relax
4 - Breathe in as you count to 4
7 - Hold your breath as you count to 7
8 - Breathe out as you count to 8

~Dr. Andrew Weil

Edith Widder: How we found the giant squid (9 minutes)
TED Talk

1. What can scare creatures away down in the ocean?

2. What kind of creature was the bluelight on the camera supposed to imitate?

3. What is the size of the squid comparable to?

4. How much of the ocean has been explored?

5. What does Edith Widder advocate for in her talk?

David Gallo: Underwater astonishments (5 minutes)

TED Talk

1. What are some things deepwater creatures can create with neon color?

2. Describe how a cephalopod can change to match the environment.

3. & 4. What are 2 things an octopus can change to match his surroundings?

CNN 10 STUDENT NEWS **(10 minute show)** *Write 5 things you learned from the news today.*

1. _____

2. _____

3. _____

4. _____

5. _____

Daily Goals Sheet   **I can statements for each day.*
This is the list of things that I want to accomplish (complete) today in class.

Tasks or assignments I need to complete in class *I can exercise strategies like deep breathing (4-7-8 breathing) to calm or focus myself.	Completed? Check if "yes"
1. Entry journal prompt response & daily gratitude statement *I can recognize what I value and appreciate. *I can write a thoughtful & clear response to a writing prompt.	
2. Daily Goals Sheet filled out *I can plan short-term goals in order to reach my long term goals.	
3. CNN Student News Guided Notes 1-5 *I can summarize events in a news story.	
4. Close Reading/Literacy Activity: Today we are_____ *I can complete a close reading or literacy strategy for something that I read. *I can organize and summarize information.	
Write your own goals for your school work for #s 5 and 6.	
5.	

6. *I can complete activities & lessons in my courses.	
7. Reflection sheet on goals today *I can reflect on my day and write honestly about whether or not I accomplished my short-term goals.	

In class today, my behavior goals are… Write your own personal goals for #s 3 & 4 *I can use strategies to maintain positive behaviors & reduce negative behaviors.	Did I …? Check if "yes"
1. I will keep a growth mindset.	
2. I will make healthy choices.	
3.	
4.	

DAILY REFLECTION

Explain what you did well today in at least one complete sentence. _____
_____

Explain how you would rate your performance in class today on a scale of 10 to 1, and explain why you ranked yourself that way. 10= I did my best 5= I tried half the time 1=I did not try at all
_____
_____

Write a complete sentence about one part of your work in class you would like to improve and explain why.
_____
_____

Choose to complete at least ONE of the writing prompts below. Circle which one you are completing.
1. I wish you would have known today that I…
2. I am really proud that today I…
3. My favorite part of today was…
4. I wonder if today I could...

_____
_____

Created by **Melissa Marini Švigelj-Smith** 2017-2019

Name_____ Date_____

Write one thing that you are grateful (**thankful**) for today. Finding things to be thankful for helps improve our overall happiness. Happier people are more successful people._____
_____

Today I am thankful for laughter.
Remember to practice 4-7-8 breathing as needed, and to keep a growth mindset.

> **Develop a GROWTH MINDSET -** People who believe their talents can be developed *(through hard work, good strategies & input from others)* have a growth mindset. They tend to achieve more than those with a fixed mindset. ~Dr. Carol Dweck

Instead of thinking...	Try thinking...
I give up	I won't stop until I succeed
I'm not good at this	How can I get better?
I can't be any better	I can always improve
This is too hard	This may take some time
I can't do this	I am going to learn to do this
My mistakes ruined me	I can learn from my mistakes
My plan didn't work	I can try another plan
I'm not smart	I can always learn new things
I'm jealous	I can learn from their success

4-7-8 Breathing
Use this strategy to help you stay calm & to relax
4 - Breathe in as you count to 4
7 - Hold your breath as you count to 7
8 - Breathe out as you count to 8

~Dr. Andrew Weil

[The Human Stories Behind Mass Incarceration TED Talk (13:39 minutes)](#)

1. How long has Sheila's son been in prison for a crime he didn't commit?
2. What did eyewitnesses in McKinley's case come forward to say after the district attorney was convicted?
3. Why do some people accept a plea deal even though they may be innocent of committing any crime?
4. What advice did Kortney's aunt give her in addition to "love and protection?"
5. How does mass incarceration create more crime?
6. What is the first step towards action according to one congregant?
7. How do prosecutors play a large role in the criminal justice system?

8. How is the process weighed against defendants?

CNN 10 STUDENT NEWS **(10 minute show)** *Write 5 things you learned from the news today.*

1. _____

2. _____

3. _____

4. _____

5. _____

Daily Goals Sheet   **I can statements for each day.*
This is the list of things that I want to accomplish (complete) today in class.

Tasks or assignments I need to complete in class *I can exercise strategies like deep breathing (4-7-8 breathing) to calm or focus myself.	Completed? Check if "yes"
1. Entry journal prompt response & daily gratitude statement *I can recognize what I value and appreciate. *I can write a thoughtful & clear response to a writing prompt.	
2. Daily Goals Sheet filled out *I can plan short-term goals in order to reach my long term goals.	
3. CNN Student News Guided Notes 1-5 *I can summarize events in a news story.	
4. Close Reading/Literacy Activity: Today we are_____ _____ *I can complete a close reading or literacy strategy for something that I read. *I can organize and summarize information.	
Write your own goals for your school work for #s 5 and 6.	
5.	
6. *I can complete activities & lessons in my courses.	

Created by Melissa Marini Švigelj-Smith 2017-2019

7. Reflection sheet on goals today *I can reflect on my day and write honestly about whether or not I accomplished my short-term goals.	

In class today, my behavior goals are… Write your own personal goals for #s 3 & 4 *I can use strategies to maintain positive behaviors & reduce negative behaviors.	Did I …? Check if "yes"
1. I will keep a growth mindset.	
2. I will make healthy choices.	
3.	
4.	

"Education then, beyond all other devices of human origin,

Is a great equalizer of the conditions of men." – Horace Mann, 1848.

DAILY REFLECTION

Explain what you did well today in at least one complete sentence. _____
_____

Explain how you would rate your performance in class today on a scale of 10 to 1, and explain why you ranked yourself that way. 10= I did my best 5= I tried half the time 1=I did not try at all
_____
_____

Write a complete sentence about one part of your work in class you would like to improve and explain why.
_____
_____

Choose to complete at least ONE of the writing prompts below. Circle which one you are completing.
1. I wish that you would have known today that I…
2. I am really proud that today I…
3. My favorite part of today was…
4. I wonder if today I could...
_____
_____
_____

Created by **Melissa Marini Švigelj-Smith** 2017-2019

Name_____Date_____

Write one thing you are grateful (**thankful**) for today. Finding things to be thankful for helps improve our overall happiness. Happier people are more successful people._____
_____

Today I am thankful for ears to hear.

Remember to practice 4-7-8 breathing as needed, and to keep a growth mindset.

> **Develop a *GROWTH MINDSET*** - *People who believe their talents can be developed (through hard work, good strategies & input from others) have a growth mindset. They tend to achieve more than those with a fixed mindset. ~Dr. Carol Dweck*

4-7-8 Breathing
Use this strategy to help you stay calm & to relax
4 - Breathe in as you count to 4
7 - Hold your breath as you count to 7
8 - Breathe out as you count to 8

~Dr. Andrew Weil

Instead of thinking...	Try thinking...
I give up	I won't stop until I succeed
I'm not good at this	How can I get better?
I can't be any better	I can always improve
This is too hard	This may take some time
I can't do this	I am going to learn to do this
My mistakes ruined me	I can learn from my mistakes
My plan didn't work	I can try another plan
I'm not smart	I can always learn new things
I'm jealous	I can learn from their success

[It's Your Turn to Listen?](#) **Deonta Bell (9 minutes)**

1. What was a challenge Deonta had growing up?

2. Why didn't JB really have it better than Deonta, even though Deonta thought he did at the time?

3. What was Deonta's main goal during his first adult prison sentence?

4. What happened when Deonta got home?

5. What does Deonta suggest that adults should do in order to help struggling youth?

CNN 10 STUDENT NEWS (**10 minute show**) *Write 5 things you learned from the news today.*

1. _____
   _____
2. _____
   _____
3. _____
   _____
4. _____
   _____
5. _____
   _____

Daily Goals Sheet   *****I can statements for each day.**
This is the list of things that I want to accomplish (complete) today in class.

Tasks or assignments I need to complete in class *I can exercise strategies like deep breathing (4-7-8 breathing) to calm or focus myself.	Completed? Check if "yes"
1. Entry journal prompt response & daily gratitude statement *I can recognize what I value and appreciate. *I can write a thoughtful & clear response to a writing prompt.	
2. Daily Goals Sheet filled out *I can plan short-term goals in order to reach my long term goals.	
3. CNN Student News Guided Notes 1-5 *I can summarize events in a news story.	
4. Close Reading/Literacy Activity: Today we are_____ *I can complete a close reading or literacy strategy for something that I read. *I can organize and summarize information.	
Write your own goals for your school work for #s 5 and 6.	
5.	
6. *I can complete activities & lessons in my courses.	
7. Reflection sheet on goals today *I can reflect on my day and write honestly about whether or not I	

Created by **Melissa Marini Švigelj-Smith** 2017-2019

| accomplished my short-term goals. | |

In class today, my behavior goals are… Write your own personal goals for #s 3 & 4 *I can use strategies to maintain positive behaviors & reduce negative behaviors.	Did I …? Check if "yes"
1. I will keep a growth mindset.	
2. I will make healthy choices.	
3.	
4.	

DAILY REFLECTION

Explain what you did well today in at least one complete sentence. _____
_____

Explain how you would rate your performance in class today on a scale of 10 to 1, and explain why you ranked yourself that way. 10= I did my best 5= I tried half the time 1=I did not try at all
_____
_____

Write a complete sentence about one part of your work in class you would like to improve and explain why.
_____
_____

Choose to complete at least ONE of the writing prompts below. Circle which one you are completing.
1. I wish that you would have known today that I…
2. I am really proud that today I…
3. My favorite part of today was…
4. I wonder if today I could...

_____
_____

Created by **Melissa Marini Švigelj-Smith** 2017-2019

Name_____Date_____

Write one thing you are grateful (**thankful**) for today. Finding things to be thankful for helps improve our overall happiness. Happier people are more successful people._____
_____

Today, I am thankful for changing seasons.

Remember to practice 4-7-8 breathing as needed, and to keep a growth mindset.

Develop a *GROWTH MINDSET* - People who believe their talents can be developed (through hard work, good strategies & input from others) have a growth mindset. They tend to achieve more than those with a fixed mindset. ~Dr. Carol Dweck

Instead of thinking...	Try thinking...
I give up	I won't stop until I succeed
I'm not good at this	How can I get better?
I can't be any better	I can always improve
This is too hard	This may take some time
I can't do this	I am going to learn to do this
My mistakes ruined me	I can learn from my mistakes
My plan didn't work	I can try another plan
I'm not smart	I can always learn new things
I'm jealous	I can learn from their success

~Dr. Andrew Weil

[Joe Ehrmann: Be A Man](#) **(14 minutes)**

1. - 3. What are 3 myths of masculinity?

4. What is alexithymia?

5. What is something men become addicted to in order to deal with emotions?

6. & 7. What should be the 2 driving forces for manhood?

8. Where is a good place to start redefining manhood?

9. What should happen when someone sees a young boy crying?

Created by **Melissa Marini Švigelj-Smith** 2017-2019

CNN 10 STUDENT NEWS (10 minute show) *Write 5 things you learned from the news today.*

1. _____
   _____
   _____

2. _____
   _____
   _____

3. _____
   _____
   _____

4. _____
   _____
   _____

5. _____
   _____
   _____

Daily Goals Sheet *I can statements for each day.*
This is the list of things that I want to accomplish (complete) today in class.

Tasks or assignments I need to complete in class *I can exercise strategies like deep breathing (4-7-8 breathing) to calm or focus myself.	Completed? Check if "yes"
1. Entry journal prompt response & daily gratitude statement *I can recognize what I value and appreciate. *I can write a thoughtful & clear response to a writing prompt.	
2. Daily Goals Sheet filled out *I can plan short-term goals in order to reach my long term goals.	
3. CNN Student News Guided Notes 1-5 *I can summarize events in a news story.	
4. Close Reading/Literacy Activity: Today we are_____ _____ *I can complete a close reading or literacy strategy for something that I read. *I can organize and summarize information.	
Write your own goals for your school work for #s 5 and 6.	
5.	
6. *I can complete activities & lessons in my courses.	
7. Reflection sheet on goals today	

Created by **Melissa Marini Švigelj-Smith** 2017-2019

*I can reflect on my day and write honestly about whether or not I accomplished my short-term goals.	

In class today, my behavior goals are... Write your own personal goals for #s 3 & 4 *I can use strategies to maintain positive behaviors & reduce negative behaviors.	Did I ...? Check if "yes"
1. I will keep a growth mindset.	
2. I will make healthy choices.	
3.	
4.	

DAILY REFLECTION

Explain what you did well today in at least one complete sentence. _____
_____
_____

Explain how you would rate your performance in class today on a scale of 10 to 1, and explain why you ranked yourself that way. 10= I did my best 5= I tried half the time 1=I did not try at all
_____
_____
_____

Write a complete sentence about one part of your work in class you would like to improve and explain why.
_____
_____
_____

Choose to complete at least ONE of the writing prompts below. Circle which one you are completing.
1. I wish you would have known today that I…
2. I am really proud that today I…
3. My favorite part of today was…
4. I wonder if today I could...

_____
_____
_____

Created by **Melissa Marini Švigelj-Smith** 2017-2019

Name_____Date_____

Write one thing you are grateful (**thankful**) for today. Finding things to be thankful for helps improve our overall happiness. Happier people are more successful people._____
_____

Today I am thankful for people who forgive.

Remember to practice 4-7-8 breathing as needed, and to keep a growth mindset.

Develop a *GROWTH MINDSET* - *People who believe their talents can be developed (through hard work, good strategies & input from others) have a growth mindset. They tend to achieve more than those with a fixed mindset. ~Dr. Carol Dweck*

Instead of thinking...	Try thinking...
I give up	I won't stop until I succeed
I'm not good at this	How can I get better?
I can't be any better	I can always improve
This is too hard	This may take some time
I can't do this	I am going to learn to do this
My mistakes ruined me	I can learn from my mistakes
My plan didn't work	I can try another plan
I'm not smart	I can always learn new things
I'm jealous	I can learn from their success

4-7-8 Breathing
Use this strategy to help you stay calm & to relax
4 - Breathe in as you count to 4
7 - Hold your breath as you count to 7
8 - Breathe out as you count to 8

~Dr. Andrew Weil

[John Legend - Redemption](#) **Song TED Talk (9 minutes)**

1. - 3. What are the core values that John Legend believes should guide our society?

4. John Legend states that we are all worthy of _____.

5. What is the theme (message) of James Cavitt's poem "Where I Live?"

6. What is the mood or tone of the song "Redemption" by Bob Marley that John Legend sings?

Created by **Melissa Marini Švigelj-Smith** 2017-2019

CNN 10 STUDENT NEWS (10 minute show) *Write 5 things you learned from the news today.*

1. _____
_____
_____

2. _____
_____
_____

3. _____
_____
_____

4. _____
_____
_____

5. _____
_____
_____

Daily Goals Sheet   *****I can statements for each day.**
This is the list of things that I want to accomplish (complete) today in class.

Tasks or assignments I need to complete in class *I can exercise strategies like deep breathing (4-7-8 breathing) to calm or focus myself.	Completed? Check if "yes"
1. Entry journal prompt response & daily gratitude statement *I can recognize what I value and appreciate. *I can write a thoughtful & clear response to a writing prompt.	
2. Daily Goals Sheet filled out *I can plan short-term goals in order to reach my long term goals.	
3. CNN Student News Guided Notes 1-5 *I can summarize events in a news story.	
4. Close Reading/Literacy Activity: Today we are_____ _____ *I can complete a close reading or literacy strategy for something that I read. *I can organize and summarize information.	
Write your own goals for your school work for #s 5 and 6.	
5.	
6. *I can complete activities & lessons in my courses.	
7. Reflection sheet on goals today *I can reflect on my day and write honestly about whether or not I	

accomplished my short-term goals.	

In class today, my behavior goals are... **Write your own personal goals for #s 3 & 4** *I can use strategies to maintain positive behaviors & reduce negative behaviors.	**Did I ...? Check if "yes"**
1. I will keep a growth mindset.	
2. I will make healthy choices.	
3.	
4.	

DAILY REFLECTION

Explain what you did well today in at least one complete sentence. ______________________

____

____

Explain how you would rate your performance in class today on a scale of 10 to 1, and explain why you ranked yourself that way. 10= I did my best 5= I tried half the time 1=I did not try at all

____

____

____

Write a complete sentence about one part of your work in class you would like to improve and explain why.

____

____

____

Choose to complete at least ONE of the writing prompts below. Circle which one you are completing.

1. I wish you would have known today that I…
2. I am really proud that today I…
3. My favorite part of today was…
4. I wonder if today I could...

____

____

____

Name_____Date_____

Write one thing you are grateful (**thankful**) for today. Finding things to be thankful for helps improve our overall happiness. Happier people are more successful people._____

_____

Today I am thankful for siblings!

Remember to practice 4-7-8 breathing as needed, and to keep a growth mindset.

> **Develop a *GROWTH MINDSET* -** *People who believe their talents can be developed (through hard work, good strategies & input from others) have a growth mindset. They tend to achieve more than those with a fixed mindset. ~Dr. Carol Dweck*

Instead of thinking...	Try thinking...
I give up	I won't stop until I succeed
I'm not good at this	How can I get better?
I can't be any better	I can always improve
This is too hard	This may take some time
I can't do this	I am going to learn to do this
My mistakes ruined me	I can learn from my mistakes
My plan didn't work	I can try another plan
I'm not smart	I can always learn new things
I'm jealous	I can learn from their success

Jose Miguel Sokoloff: How Christmas Lights Helped Guerrillas Put Down Their Guns
(14 minute TED Talk)

1. Which country is Mr. Sokoloff talking about?

2. How did Christmas Lights help demobilize the guerrilla fighters?

3. How could the guerrillas in the jungle hear the 100 stories that were recorded?

4. How long did Giovanni walk in order to find the girl that he loved?

5. What did Captain Valdez say that being generous did for him and for his men?

6. What are the highways of the jungle?

7. How did the fears of the guerrillas change as the peace process continued?

8. Who else got involved in trying to get the guerrillas to come home?

9. How many Colombian guerrillas demobilized over eight years?

CNN 10 STUDENT NEWS (10 minute show) *Write 5 things you learned from the news today.*

1. _____
   _____
   _____

2. _____
   _____
   _____

3. _____
   _____
   _____

4. _____
   _____
   _____

5. _____
   _____
   _____

Daily Goals Sheet *I can statements for each day.*
This is the list of things that I want to accomplish (complete) today in class.

Tasks or assignments I need to complete in class *I can exercise strategies like deep breathing (4-7-8 breathing) to calm or focus myself.	Completed? Check if "yes"
1. Entry journal prompt response & daily gratitude statement *I can recognize what I value and appreciate. *I can write a thoughtful & clear response to a writing prompt.	
2. Daily Goals Sheet filled out *I can plan short-term goals in order to reach my long term goals.	
3. CNN Student News Guided Notes 1-5 *I can summarize events in a news story.	
4. Close Reading/Literacy Activity: Today we are_____ _____ *I can complete a close reading or literacy strategy for something that I read. *I can organize and summarize information.	
Write your own goals for your school work for #s 5 and 6.	

5.	
6. *I can complete activities & lessons in my courses.	
7. Reflection sheet on goals today *I can reflect on my day and write honestly about whether or not I accomplished my short-term goals.	

In class today, my behavior goals are… Write your own personal goals for #s 3 & 4 *I can use strategies to maintain positive behaviors & reduce negative behaviors.	Did I …? Check if "yes"
1. I will keep a growth mindset.	
2. I will make healthy choices.	
3.	
4.	

DAILY REFLECTION

Explain what you did well today in at least one complete sentence. _____
_____

Explain how you would rate your performance in class today on a scale of 10 to 1, and explain why you ranked yourself that way. 10= I did my best 5= I tried half the time 1=I did not try at all
_____
_____

Write a complete sentence about one part of your work in class you would like to improve and explain why.
_____
_____

Choose to complete at least ONE of the writing prompts below. Circle which one you are completing.
1. I wish you would have known today that I…
2. I am really proud that today I…
3. My favorite part of today was…
4. I wonder if today I could...

_____
_____
_____

Name_____ Date_____

Write one thing you are grateful (**thankful**) for today. Finding things to be thankful for helps improve our overall happiness. Happier people are more successful people._____
_____

Today, I am thankful for my thumbs.

Remember to practice 4-7-8 breathing as needed, and to keep a growth mindset.

> **Develop a *GROWTH MINDSET* -** *People who believe their talents can be developed (through hard work, good strategies & input from others) have a growth mindset. They tend to achieve more than those with a fixed mindset. ~Dr. Carol Dweck*

Instead of thinking...	Try thinking...
I give up	I won't stop until I succeed
I'm not good at this	How can I get better?
I can't be any better	I can always improve
This is too hard	This may take some time
I can't do this	I am going to learn to do this
My mistakes ruined me	I can learn from my mistakes
My plan didn't work	I can try another plan
I'm not smart	I can always learn new things
I'm jealous	I can learn from their success

4-7-8 Breathing
Use this strategy to help you stay calm & to relax
4 - Breathe in as you count to 4
7 - Hold your breath as you count to 7
8 - Breathe out as you count to 8

~Dr. Andrew Weil

[Josh Luber:The secret sneaker market — and why it matters](#) (12 minute TED Talk)

Answer the questions as you watch the video.

1. What shoe may have saved Nike?

2. How much are "Back to the Future" sneakers?

3. Why did one man think his son was selling drugs?

4. Who is making the rules in the sneaker market?

Created by **Melissa Marini Švigelj-Smith** 2017-2019

5. Nike sets the rules by controlling the

_____

6. What do you think would be a good item for a stock market of things?

CNN 10 STUDENT NEWS (**10 minute show**) *Write **5** things you learned from the news today.*

1. _____
   _____
   _____

2. _____
   _____
   _____

3. _____
   _____
   _____

4. _____
   _____
   _____

5. _____
   _____
   _____

Daily Goals Sheet   **I can statements for each day.*
This is the list of things that I want to accomplish (complete) today in class.

Tasks or assignments I need to complete in class *I can exercise strategies like deep breathing (4-7-8 breathing) to calm or focus myself.	Completed? Check if "yes"
1. Entry journal prompt response & daily gratitude statement *I can recognize what I value and appreciate. *I can write a thoughtful & clear response to a writing prompt.	
2. Daily Goals Sheet filled out *I can plan short-term goals in order to reach my long term goals.	
3. CNN Student News Guided Notes 1-5 *I can summarize events in a news story.	
4. Close Reading/Literacy Activity: Today we are_____ _____ *I can complete a close reading or literacy strategy for something that I read. *I can organize and summarize information.	
Write your own goals for your school work for #s 5 and 6.	
5.	

Created by **Melissa Marini Švigelj-Smith** 2017-2019

6. *I can complete activities & lessons in my courses.	
7. Reflection sheet on goals today *I can reflect on my day and write honestly about whether or not I accomplished my short-term goals.	

In class today, my behavior goals are… Write your own personal goals for #s 3 & 4 *I can use strategies to maintain positive behaviors & reduce negative behaviors.	Did I …? Check if "yes"
1. I will keep a growth mindset.	
2. I will make healthy choices.	
3.	
4.	

DAILY REFLECTION

Explain what you did well today in at least one complete sentence. _____
_____
_____

Explain how you would rate your performance in class today on a scale of 10 to 1, and explain why you ranked yourself that way. 10= I did my best 5= I tried half the time 1=I did not try at all
_____
_____

Write a complete sentence about one part of your work in class you would like to improve and explain why.
_____
_____

Choose to complete at least ONE of the writing prompts below. Circle which one you are completing.
1. I wish you would have known today that I…
2. I am really proud that today I…
3. My favorite part of today was…
4. I wonder if today I could...
_____
_____

Created by **Melissa Marini Švigelj-Smith** 2017-2019

Name_____Date_____

Write one thing you are grateful **(thankful)** for today. Finding things to be thankful for helps improve our overall happiness. Happier people are more successful people._____
_____

Today I am thankful for creatures big and small.

Remember to practice 4-7-8 breathing as needed, and to keep a growth mindset.

Develop a *GROWTH MINDSET* - People who believe their talents can be developed (through hard work, good strategies & input from others) have a growth mindset. They tend to achieve more than those with a fixed mindset. ~Dr. Carol Dweck

Instead of thinking...	Try thinking...
I give up	I won't stop until I succeed
I'm not good at this	How can I get better?
I can't be any better	I can always improve
This is too hard	This may take some time
I can't do this	I am going to learn to do this
My mistakes ruined me	I can learn from my mistakes
My plan didn't work	I can try another plan
I'm not smart	I can always learn new things
I'm jealous	I can learn from their success

4-7-8 Breathing
Use this strategy to help you stay calm & to relax
4 - Breathe in as you count to 4
7 - Hold your breath as you count to 7
8 - Breathe out as you count to 8

~Dr. Andrew Weil

TED Talk - Laurel Braitman
Depressed Dogs, Cats with OCD - What we can learn about humans from animals
(20 minutes)

1. What 2 things are the majority of mental disorders related to?

2. Name 2 things that animals are doing that could be considered disorders or mental health issues.

3. How did a one-armed animal move from being depressed to very happy?

4. What did Bonobo in Milwaukee start doing with his prescription medication?

5. What seems to help animals the most?

Created by **Melissa Marini Švigelj-Smith** 2017-2019

6. How has Dr. Braitman's research changed her?

7. What things have you learned or could you learn that could help make you a more caring person?

CNN 10 STUDENT NEWS (10 minute show) *Write 5 things you learned from the news today.*

1. _____

2. _____

3. _____

4. _____

5. _____

Daily Goals Sheet **I can statements for each day.*
This is the list of things that I want to accomplish (complete) today in class.

Tasks or assignments I need to complete in class *I can exercise strategies like deep breathing (4-7-8 breathing) to calm or focus myself.	Completed? Check if "yes"
1. Entry journal prompt response & daily gratitude statement *I can recognize what I value and appreciate. *I can write a thoughtful & clear response to a writing prompt.	
2. Daily Goals Sheet filled out *I can plan short-term goals in order to reach my long term goals.	
3. CNN Student News Guided Notes 1-5 *I can summarize events in a news story.	
4. Close Reading/Literacy Activity: Today we are_____ *I can complete a close reading or literacy strategy for something that I read. *I can organize and summarize information.	
Write your own goals for your school work for #s 5 and 6.	
5.	

6. *I can complete activities & lessons in my courses.	
7. Reflection sheet on goals today *I can reflect on my day and write honestly about whether or not I accomplished my short-term goals.	

In class today, my behavior goals are… Write your own personal goals for #s 3 & 4 *I can use strategies to maintain positive behaviors & reduce negative behaviors.	Did I …? Check if "yes"
1. I will keep a growth mindset.	
2. I will make healthy choices.	
3.	
4.	

DAILY REFLECTION

Explain what you did well today in at least one complete sentence. _____
_____

Explain how you would rate your performance in class today on a scale of 10 to 1, and explain why you ranked yourself that way. 10= I did my best 5= I tried half the time 1=I did not try at all
_____
_____

Write a complete sentence about one part of your work in class you would like to improve and explain why.
_____
_____

Choose to complete at least ONE of the writing prompts below. Circle which one you are completing.
1. I wish you would have known today that I…
2. I am really proud that today I…
3. My favorite part of today was…
4. I wonder if today I could...

_____
_____
_____

Created by **Melissa Marini Švigelj-Smith** 2017-2019

Name_____Date_____

Write one thing you are grateful (**thankful**) for today. Finding things to be thankful for helps improve our overall happiness. Happier people are more successful people._____
_____

Today I am thankful for raindrops.
Remember to practice 4-7-8 breathing as needed, and to keep a growth mindset.

> **Develop a *GROWTH MINDSET*** - *People who believe their talents can be developed (through hard work, good strategies & input from others) have a growth mindset. They tend to achieve more than those with a fixed mindset. ~Dr. Carol Dweck*

Instead of thinking...	Try thinking...
I give up	I won't stop until I succeed
I'm not good at this	How can I get better?
I can't be any better	I can always improve
This is too hard	This may take some time
I can't do this	I am going to learn to do this
My mistakes ruined me	I can learn from my mistakes
My plan didn't work	I can try another plan
I'm not smart	I can always learn new things
I'm jealous	I can learn from their success

~Dr. Andrew Weil

[Life Lessons from an Incarcerated Father: Last Chance High Episode 6](#) (12 minutes)

1. Which state is Cortez visiting his dad in?

2. How long has it been since Cortez visited with his dad?

3. - 5. List 3 bits of advice that Cortez's father offers him.

6. How did Cortez's visit seem to impact him according to adults?

Created by **Melissa Marini Švigelj-Smith** 2017-2019

CNN 10 STUDENT NEWS (**10 minute show**) *Write 5 things you learned from the news today.*

1. _____
   _____
   _____

2. _____
   _____
   _____

3. _____
   _____
   _____

4. _____
   _____
   _____

5. _____
   _____
   _____

Daily Goals Sheet   ***I can statements for each day.**
This is the list of things that I want to accomplish (complete) today in class.

Tasks or assignments I need to complete in class *I can exercise strategies like deep breathing (4-7-8 breathing) to calm or focus myself.	Completed? Check if "yes"
1. Entry journal prompt response & daily gratitude statement *I can recognize what I value and appreciate. *I can write a thoughtful & clear response to a writing prompt.	
2. Daily Goals Sheet filled out *I can plan short-term goals in order to reach my long term goals.	
3. CNN Student News Guided Notes 1-5 *I can summarize events in a news story.	
4. Close Reading/Literacy Activity: Today we are_____ *I can complete a close reading or literacy strategy for something that I read. *I can organize and summarize information.	
Write your own goals for your school work for #s 5 and 6.	
5.	
6. *I can complete activities & lessons in my courses.	
7. Reflection sheet on goals today	

Created by **Melissa Marini Švigelj-Smith** 2017-2019

	Did I...? Check if "yes"
*I can reflect on my day and write honestly about whether or not I accomplished my short-term goals.	

In class today, my behavior goals are... **Write your own personal goals for #s 3 & 4** *I can use strategies to maintain positive behaviors & reduce negative behaviors.	**Did I ...?** **Check if "yes"**
1. I will keep a growth mindset.	
2. I will make healthy choices.	
3.	
4.	

DAILY REFLECTION

Explain what you did well today in at least one complete sentence. _____
_____

Explain how you would rate your performance in class today on a scale of 10 to 1, and explain why you ranked yourself that way. 10= I did my best 5= I tried half the time 1=I did not try at all
_____
_____

Write a complete sentence about one part of your work in class you would like to improve and explain why.
_____
_____

Choose to complete at least ONE of the writing prompts below. Circle which one you are completing.
1. I wish you would have known today that I...
2. I am really proud that today I...
3. My favorite part of today was...
4. I wonder if today I could...

_____
_____
_____

Name_____ Date_____

Write one thing you are grateful (**thankful**) for today. Finding things to be thankful for helps improve our overall happiness. Happier people are more successful people._____
_____

Today I am thankful for autumn colors.

Remember to practice 4-7-8 breathing as needed, and to keep a growth mindset.

> **Develop a *GROWTH MINDSET* -** *People who believe their talents can be developed (through hard work, good strategies & input from others) have a growth mindset. They tend to achieve more than those with a fixed mindset. ~Dr. Carol Dweck*

Instead of thinking...	Try thinking...
I give up	I won't stop until I succeed
I'm not good at this	How can I get better?
I can't be any better	I can always improve
This is too hard	This may take some time
I can't do this	I am going to learn to do this
My mistakes ruined me	I can learn from my mistakes
My plan didn't work	I can try another plan
I'm not smart	I can always learn new things
I'm jealous	I can learn from their success

4-7-8 Breathing
Use this strategy to help you stay calm & to relax
4 - Breathe in as you count to 4
7 - Hold your breath as you count to 7
8 - Breathe out as you count to 8

~Dr. Andrew Weil

<u>Lift Off</u>, as you listen to Donovan Livingston at his Harvard graduation, fill in the blanks below. Then, answer the questions.
<u>https://www.gse.harvard.edu/news/16/05/lift</u> *(4 minutes)*

1. For generations we have known of knowledge's _____ power.
2. But I've always been a thorn in the side of _____.
3. My past, alone won't allow me to _____ still.
4. Keep _____. Grab them.
5. At the core, none of us were meant to be _____.
6. Together, we can inspire galaxies of _____

    For generations to come.

Created by **Melissa Marini Švigelj-Smith** 2017-2019

7. What kind of literary devices are used in the poem? Alliteration? Personification? Simile? Metaphor?

8. What is the mood or tone of this poem?

9. What is the theme or message of the poem?

10. Use the text to support your answer to the previous question. Which words in the poem helped you identify or understand the message or theme?

CNN 10 STUDENT NEWS (10 minute show) *Write 5 things you learned from the news today.*

1. _____

2. _____

3. _____

4. _____

5. _____

Daily Goals Sheet *** I can statements for each day.**
This is the list of things that I want to accomplish (complete) today in class.

Tasks or assignments I need to complete in class *I can exercise strategies like deep breathing (4-7-8 breathing) to calm or focus myself.	Completed? Check if "yes"
1. Entry journal prompt response & daily gratitude statement *I can recognize what I value and appreciate. *I can write a thoughtful & clear response to a writing prompt.	
2. Daily Goals Sheet filled out *I can plan short-term goals in order to reach my long term goals.	
3. CNN Student News Guided Notes 1-5 *I can summarize events in a news story.	
4. Close Reading/Literacy Activity: Today we are_____	

Created by **Melissa Marini Švigelj-Smith** 2017-2019

*I can complete a close reading or literacy strategy for something that I read. *I can organize and summarize information.	
Write your own goals for your school work for #s 5 and 6.	
5.	
6. *I can complete activities & lessons in my courses.	
7. Reflection sheet on goals today *I can reflect on my day and write honestly about whether or not I accomplished my short-term goals.	

In class today, my behavior goals are… **Write your own personal goals for #s 3 & 4** *I can use strategies to maintain positive behaviors & reduce negative behaviors.	**Did I …?** **Check if "yes"**
1. I will keep a growth mindset.	
2. I will make healthy choices.	
3.	
4.	

"Education then, beyond all other devices of human origin,

Is a great equalizer of the conditions of men." – Horace Mann, 1848.

Daily reflection is on the next page today.

DAILY REFLECTION

Explain what you did well today in at least one complete sentence. _____
_____
_____

Explain how you would rate your performance in class today on a scale of 10 to 1, and explain why you ranked yourself that way. 10= I did my best 5= I tried half the time 1=I did not try at all
_____
_____
_____

Write a complete sentence about one part of your work in class you would like to improve and explain why.
_____
_____
_____

Choose to complete at least ONE of the writing prompts below. Circle which one you are completing.
1. I wish you would have known today that I…
2. I am really proud that today I…
3. My favorite part of today was…
4. I wonder if today I could...

_____
_____
_____

Name_____Date_____

Write one thing you are grateful (**thankful**) for today. Finding things to be thankful for helps improve our overall happiness. Happier people are more successful people. _____

_____

Today I'm thankful I'm here!

Remember to practice 4-7-8 breathing as needed, and to keep a growth mindset.

> **Develop a GROWTH MINDSET -** *People who believe their talents can be developed (through hard work, good strategies & input from others) have a growth mindset. They tend to achieve more than those with a fixed mindset. ~Dr. Carol Dweck*

Instead of thinking...	Try thinking...
I give up	I won't stop until I succeed
I'm not good at this	How can I get better?
I can't be any better	I can always improve
This is too hard	This may take some time
I can't do this	I am going to learn to do this
My mistakes ruined me	I can learn from my mistakes
My plan didn't work	I can try another plan
I'm not smart	I can always learn new things
I'm jealous	I can learn from their success

4-7-8 Breathing
Use this strategy to help you stay calm & to relax
4 - Breathe in as you count to 4
7 - Hold your breath as you count to 7
8 - Breathe out as you count to 8

~Dr. Andrew Weil

[Marshall Davis Jones: Spelling Father](#) **on Vimeo (3.5 mins)**

1. Which poetic device(s) does the poet use in his poem (alliteration, personification, simile, metaphor, rhyme, etc.)?

_____

_____

2. Cite an example of a literary or poetic device used in the text (poem words).

_____

_____

3. What is the mood or tone of the poem? Where does the poem's mood shift or change?

_____

_____

4. What is the message of the poem? What does the author want us to learn or think about?

_____

_____

Created by **Melissa Marini Švigelj-Smith** 2017-2019

5. What title would you give this poem instead of "Spelling Father"? _____
_____

CNN 10 STUDENT NEWS **(10 minute show)** *Write 5 things you learned from the news today.*

1. _____
   _____
   _____

2. _____
   _____
   _____

3. _____
   _____
   _____

4. _____
   _____
   _____

5. _____
   _____
   _____

Daily Goals Sheet   **I can statements for each day.*
This is the list of things that I want to accomplish (complete) today in class.

Tasks or assignments I need to complete in class	Completed? Check if "yes"
*I can exercise strategies like deep breathing (4-7-8 breathing) to calm or focus myself.	
1. Entry journal prompt response & daily gratitude statement *I can recognize what I value and appreciate. *I can write a thoughtful & clear response to a writing prompt.	
2. Daily Goals Sheet filled out *I can plan short-term goals in order to reach my long term goals.	
3. CNN Student News Guided Notes 1-5 *I can summarize events in a news story.	
4. Close Reading/Literacy Activity: Today we are_____ _____ *I can complete a close reading or literacy strategy for something that I read. *I can organize and summarize information.	
Write your own goals for your school work for #s 5 and 6.	
5.	
6. *I can complete activities & lessons in my courses.	

Created by **Melissa Marini Švigelj-Smith** 2017-2019

7. Reflection sheet on goals today *I can reflect on my day and write honestly about whether or not I accomplished my short-term goals.	

In class today, my behavior goals are... **Write your own personal goals for #s 3 & 4** *I can use strategies to maintain positive behaviors & reduce negative behaviors.	**Did I ...?** **Check if "yes"**
1. I will keep a growth mindset.	
2. I will make healthy choices.	
3.	
4.	

DAILY REFLECTION

Explain what you did well today in at least one complete sentence
_____
_____

Explain how you would rate your performance in class today on a scale of 10 to 1, and explain why you ranked yourself that way. 10= I did my best 5= I tried half the time 1=I did not try at all
_____
_____
_____

Write a complete sentence about one part of your work in class you would like to improve and explain
why._____
_____
_____

Choose to complete at least ONE of the writing prompts below. Circle which one you are completing.
1. I wish you would have known today that I…
2. I am really proud that today I…
3. My favorite part of today was…
4. I wonder if today I could…

_____
_____
_____

Name_____ Date_____

Write one thing you are grateful (**thankful**) for today. Finding things to be thankful for helps improve our overall happiness. Happier people are more successful people._____
_____

Today I am thankful for the smell of flowers.
Remember to practice 4-7-8 breathing as needed, and to keep a growth mindset.

> **Develop a *GROWTH MINDSET* -** People who believe their talents can be developed (through hard work, good strategies & input from others) have a growth mindset. They tend to achieve more than those with a fixed mindset. ~Dr. Carol Dweck

Instead of thinking...	Try thinking...
I give up	I won't stop until I succeed
I'm not good at this	How can I get better?
I can't be any better	I can always improve
This is too hard	This may take some time
I can't do this	I am going to learn to do this
My mistakes ruined me	I can learn from my mistakes
My plan didn't work	I can try another plan
I'm not smart	I can always learn new things
I'm jealous	I can learn from their success

4-7-8 Breathing
Use this strategy to help you stay calm & to relax
4 - Breathe in as you count to 4
7 - Hold your breath as you count to 7
8 - Breathe out as you count to 8

~Dr. Andrew Weil

[Nature. Beauty. Gratitude.](#) **TED Talk (8 minutes)**
Fill in the blanks as you watch & listen to the video.

1. Flowers provide _____ of the food we eat.
2. We _____ what we fall in love with.
3. _____ percent of the information we receive comes through our eyes.
4. Nature's beauty is a gift that cultivates appreciation and _____.
5. The only appropriate response to the gift of this day that is given to you is _____.
6. Begin by opening your _____ and be surprised that you have eyes you can open.
7. Each person has an incredible _____ behind their face.

Created by **Melissa Marini Švigelj-Smith** 2017-2019

8. Open your _____ to the incredible gifts that civilization gives to us.
9. & 10. I wish you that you will open your heart to all these blessings, and let them flow through you, that everyone whom you will meet on this day will be _____ by you, just by your eyes, by your smile, by your touch, just by your presence. Let the gratefulness overflow into blessing all around you, and then it will really be a good _____.

CNN 10 STUDENT NEWS (10 minute show) *Write 5 things you learned from the news today.*

1. _____
2. _____
3. _____
4. _____
5. _____

Daily Goals Sheet *I can statements for each day.
This is the list of things that I want to accomplish (complete) today in class.

Tasks or assignments I need to complete in class *I can exercise strategies like deep breathing (4-7-8 breathing) to calm or focus myself.	Completed? Check if "yes"
1. Entry journal prompt response & daily gratitude statement *I can recognize what I value and appreciate. *I can write a thoughtful & clear response to a writing prompt.	
2. Daily Goals Sheet filled out *I can plan short-term goals in order to reach my long term goals.	
3. CNN Student News Guided Notes 1-5 *I can summarize events in a news story.	
4. Close Reading/Literacy Activity: Today we are_____ *I can complete a close reading or literacy strategy for something that I read. *I can organize and summarize information.	
Write your own goals for your school work for #s 5 and 6.	

Created by **Melissa Marini Švigelj-Smith** 2017-2019

5.	
6. *I can complete activities & lessons in my courses.	
7. Reflection sheet on goals today *I can reflect on my day and write honestly about whether or not I accomplished my short-term goals.	

In class today, my behavior goals are… **Write your own personal goals for #s 3 & 4** *I can use strategies to maintain positive behaviors & reduce negative behaviors.	**Did I …?** **Check if "yes"**
1. I will keep a growth mindset.	
2. I will make healthy choices.	
3.	
4.	

DAILY REFLECTION

Explain what you did well today in at least one complete sentence. _____
_____

Explain how you would rate your performance in class today on a scale of 10 to 1, and explain why you ranked yourself that way. 10= I did my best 5= I tried half the time 1=I did not try at all
_____
_____

Write a complete sentence about one part of your work in class you would like to improve and explain why.
_____
_____

Choose to complete at least ONE of the writing prompts below. Circle which one you are completing.
1. I wish you would have known today that I…
2. I am really proud that today I…
3. My favorite part of today was…
4. I wonder if today I could...

_____
_____

Created by **Melissa Marini Švigelj-Smith** 2017-2019

Name_____Date_____

Write one thing you are grateful (**thankful**) for today. Finding things to be thankful for helps improve our overall happiness. Happier people are more successful people._____

_____

Today I am thankful for photographs.

Remember to practice 4-7-8 breathing as needed, and to keep a growth mindset.

> **Develop a *GROWTH MINDSET* -** *People who believe their talents can be developed (through hard work, good strategies & input from others) have a growth mindset. They tend to achieve more than those with a fixed mindset. ~Dr. Carol Dweck*

Instead of thinking...	Try thinking...
I give up	I won't stop until I succeed
I'm not good at this	How can I get better?
I can't be any better	I can always improve
This is too hard	This may take some time
I can't do this	I am going to learn to do this
My mistakes ruined me	I can learn from my mistakes
My plan didn't work	I can try another plan
I'm not smart	I can always learn new things
I'm jealous	I can learn from their success

[Aaron Huey: America's Native Prisoners of War TED Talk](#) **(15 minutes)**
Answer the questions as you watch the video.

1. Where is "ground zero" for Native American issues?
2. What happened to 38 Sioux men who fought for their land in the 1860s?
3. What happened to the great warrior chief Crazy Horse?
4. What happened at the Wounded Knee Massacre in 1890?
5. In 1900 there were 250,000 Native Americans, but in 1492 there were about how many?
6. - 10. What are **5** issues, struggles, or problems that Native Americans face or that reservations confront?

A.   B.
C.   D.
E.

CNN 10 STUDENT NEWS **(10 minute show)** *Write 5 things you learned from the news today.*

1. _____
   _____
   _____

2. _____
   _____
   _____

3. _____
   _____
   _____

4. _____
   _____
   _____

5. _____
   _____
   _____

Daily Goals Sheet *I can statements for each day.
This is the list of things that I want to accomplish (complete) today in class.

Tasks or assignments I need to complete in class *I can exercise strategies like deep breathing (4-7-8 breathing) to calm or focus myself.	Completed? Check if "yes"
1. Entry journal prompt response & daily gratitude statement *I can recognize what I value and appreciate. *I can write a thoughtful & clear response to a writing prompt.	
2. Daily Goals Sheet filled out *I can plan short-term goals in order to reach my long term goals.	
3. CNN Student News Guided Notes 1-5 *I can summarize events in a news story.	
4. Close Reading/Literacy Activity: Today we are_____ _____ *I can complete a close reading or literacy strategy for something that I read. *I can organize and summarize information.	
Write your own goals for your school work for #s 5 and 6.	
5.	
6. *I can complete activities & lessons in my courses.	
7. Reflection sheet on goals today *I can reflect on my day and write honestly about whether or not I	

Created by **Melissa Marini Švigelj-Smith** 2017-2019

| accomplished my short-term goals. | |

In class today, my behavior goals are… Write your own personal goals for #s 3 & 4 *I can use strategies to maintain positive behaviors & reduce negative behaviors.	Did I …? Check if "yes"
1. I will keep a growth mindset.	
2. I will make healthy choices.	
3.	
4.	

DAILY REFLECTION

Explain what you did well today in at least one complete sentence. _____
_____

Explain how you would rate your performance in class today on a scale of 10 to 1, and explain why you ranked yourself that way. 10= I did my best 5= I tried half the time 1=I did not try at all
_____
_____

Write a complete sentence about one part of your work in class you would like to improve and explain why.
_____
_____

Choose to complete at least ONE of the writing prompts below. Circle which one you are completing.
1. I wish you would have known today that I…
2. I am really proud that today I…
3. My favorite part of today was…
4. I wonder if today I could...
_____
_____
_____

Created by **Melissa Marini Švigelj-Smith** 2017-2019

Name_____ Date_____

Write one thing you are grateful (**thankful**) for today. Finding things to be thankful for helps improve our overall happiness. Happier people are more successful people._____
_____

Today I am thankful for restoration.
Remember to practice 4-7-8 breathing as needed, and to keep a growth mindset.

> **Develop a *GROWTH MINDSET*** - *People who believe their talents can be developed (through hard work, good strategies & input from others) have a growth mindset. They tend to achieve more than those with a fixed mindset. ~Dr. Carol Dweck*

Instead of thinking...	Try thinking...
I give up	I won't stop until I succeed
I'm not good at this	How can I get better?
I can't be any better	I can always improve
This is too hard	This may take some time
I can't do this	I am going to learn to do this
My mistakes ruined me	I can learn from my mistakes
My plan didn't work	I can try another plan
I'm not smart	I can always learn new things
I'm jealous	I can learn from their success

4-7-8 Breathing
Use this strategy to help you stay calm & to relax
4 - Breathe in as you count to 4
7 - Hold your breath as you count to 7
8 - Breathe out as you count to 8

~Dr. Andrew Weil

The nightmare videos of children's YouTube TED Talk (14:30 minutes)

1. What are the 10 million videos for kids to watch showing children?
2. According to James, what do video creators get in return for hacking children's brains?
3. Which 2007 children's song spurred the creation of lots of videos with the same song tune or style?
4. Why are some YouTube videos a "meaningless mash of content and title?"
5. What are all of these algorithms and influences pulling together that parents usually don't like?
6. What advice does James give to parents with small children?
7. What is another major driver of nonsense content on YouTube?

8. Why shouldn't we leave it up to AI to decide what is appropriate or not?
9. What does Alex mean by the word "agency?"
10. What might we think of technology as instead of thinking of it as a solution?

CNN 10 STUDENT NEWS (**10 minute show**) *Write 5 things you learned from the news today.*

1. _____
_____
_____

2. _____
_____
_____

3. _____
_____
_____

4. _____
_____
_____

5. _____
_____
_____

Daily Goals Sheet   *****I can statements for each day.**
This is the list of things that I want to accomplish (complete) today in class.

Tasks or assignments I need to complete in class *I can exercise strategies like deep breathing (4-7-8 breathing) to calm or focus myself.	Completed? Check if "yes"
1. Entry journal prompt response & daily gratitude statement *I can recognize what I value and appreciate. *I can write a thoughtful & clear response to a writing prompt.	
2. Daily Goals Sheet filled out *I can plan short-term goals in order to reach my long term goals.	
3. CNN Student News Guided Notes 1-5 *I can summarize events in a news story.	
4. Close Reading/Literacy Activity: Today we are_____ _____ *I can complete a close reading or literacy strategy for something that I read. *I can organize and summarize information.	
Write your own goals for your school work for #s 5 and 6.	
5.	

6. *I can complete activities & lessons in my courses.	
7. Reflection sheet on goals today *I can reflect on my day and write honestly about whether or not I accomplished my short-term goals.	

In class today, my behavior goals are… Write your own personal goals for #s 3 & 4 *I can use strategies to maintain positive behaviors & reduce negative behaviors.	Did I …? Check if "yes"
1. I will keep a growth mindset.	
2. I will make healthy choices.	
3.	
4.	

"Education then, beyond all other devices of human origin,

Is a great equalizer of the conditions of men." – Horace Mann, 1848.

DAILY REFLECTION

Explain what you did well today in at least one complete sentence. _____
_____
_____

Explain how you would rate your performance in class today on a scale of 10 to 1, and explain why you ranked yourself that way. 10= I did my best 5= I tried half the time 1=I did not try at all
_____
_____

Write a complete sentence about one part of your work in class you would like to improve and explain why.
_____
_____

Choose to complete at least ONE of the writing prompts below. Circle which one you are completing.
1. I wish you would have known today that I…
2. I am really proud that today I…
3. My favorite part of today was…
4. I wonder if today I could...

_____
_____
_____

Name_____ Date_____

Write one thing you are grateful (**thankful**) for today. Finding things to be thankful for helps improve our overall happiness. Happier people are more successful people._____
_____

Today I am thankful for bridges.

Remember to practice 4-7-8 breathing as needed, and to keep a growth mindset.

> **Develop a *GROWTH MINDSET* -** *People who believe their talents can be developed (through hard work, good strategies & input from others) have a growth mindset. They tend to achieve more than those with a fixed mindset. ~Dr. Carol Dweck*

Instead of thinking...	Try thinking...
I give up	I won't stop until I succeed
I'm not good at this	How can I get better?
I can't be any better	I can always improve
This is too hard	This may take some time
I can't do this	I am going to learn to do this
My mistakes ruined me	I can learn from my mistakes
My plan didn't work	I can try another plan
I'm not smart	I can always learn new things
I'm jealous	I can learn from their success

4-7-8 Breathing
Use this strategy to help you stay calm & to relax
4 - Breathe in as you count to 4
7 - Hold your breath as you count to 7
8 - Breathe out as you count to 8

~Dr. Andrew Weil

An Artist's Unflinching Look at Racial Violence - TED Talk (4 minutes)

1. In Buddhism, the lotus is a symbol for transcendence and for _____ of mind and spirit.

2. I created this body of work simply entitled "_____."

3. These killings have been going on for over _____ years.

CNN 10 STUDENT NEWS (10 minute show) *Write 5 things you learned from the news today.*

1. _____
_____
2. _____
_____
_____

Created by **Melissa Marini Švigelj-Smith** 2017-2019

3. _____
_____
_____
_____

4. _____
_____
_____
_____

5. _____
_____
_____
_____

Daily Goals Sheet   *I can statements for each day.*
This is the list of things that I want to accomplish (complete) today in class.

Tasks or assignments I need to complete in class *I can exercise strategies like deep breathing (4-7-8 breathing) to calm or focus myself.	Completed? Check if "yes"
1. Entry journal prompt response & daily gratitude statement *I can recognize what I value and appreciate. *I can write a thoughtful & clear response to a writing prompt.	
2. Daily Goals Sheet filled out *I can plan short-term goals in order to reach my long term goals.	
3. CNN Student News Guided Notes 1-5 *I can summarize events in a news story.	
4. Close Reading/Literacy Activity: Today we are_____ *I can complete a close reading or literacy strategy for something that I read. *I can organize and summarize information.	
Write your own goals for your school work for #s 5 and 6.	
5.	
6. *I can complete activities & lessons in my courses.	
7. Reflection sheet on goals today *I can reflect on my day and write honestly about whether or not I accomplished my short-term goals.	

In class today, my behavior goals are… Write your own personal goals for #s 3 & 4 *I can use strategies to maintain positive behaviors & reduce negative behaviors.	Did I …? Check if "yes"

Created by Melissa Marini Švigelj-Smith 2017-2019

1. I will keep a growth mindset.	
2. I will make healthy choices.	
3.	
4.	

DAILY REFLECTION

Explain what you did well today in at least one complete sentence. _____
_____
_____

Explain how you would rate your performance in class today on a scale of 10 to 1, and explain why you ranked yourself that way. 10= I did my best 5= I tried half the time 1=I did not try at all
_____
_____
_____

Write a complete sentence about one part of your work in class you would like to improve and explain why.
_____
_____
_____

Choose to complete at least ONE of the writing prompts below. Circle which one you are completing.
1. I wish you would have known today that I…
2. I am really proud that today I…
3. My favorite part of today was…
4. I wonder if today I could...

_____
_____
_____

Name_____Date_____

Write one thing you are grateful (**thankful**) for today. Finding things to be thankful for helps improve our overall happiness. Happier people are more successful people._____
_____

Today I am thankful for restoration.
Remember to practice 4-7-8 breathing as needed, and to keep a growth mindset.

> **Develop a *GROWTH MINDSET* -** People who believe their talents can be developed (through hard work, good strategies & input from others) have a growth mindset. They tend to achieve more than those with a fixed mindset. *~Dr. Carol Dweck*

Instead of thinking...	Try thinking...
I give up	I won't stop until I succeed
I'm not good at this	How can I get better?
I can't be any better	I can always improve
This is too hard	This may take some time
I can't do this	I am going to learn to do this
My mistakes ruined me	I can learn from my mistakes
My plan didn't work	I can try another plan
I'm not smart	I can always learn new things
I'm jealous	I can learn from their success

[What a world without prisons could look like TED Talk](#) (15 minutes)

1. What does Deanna ask the audience to imagine?
2. Why did Deanna build huts in the woods behind her house when she was a child?
3. As an architect, what did Deanna notice about the prison she visited?
4. What is something restorative justice can do?
5. What do suspensions and expulsions often do?
6. What did Danny design?
7. What was the Center for Court Innovative Practices doing?
8. What is Restore Oakland going to be?
9. How many restorative justice centers can be built for the cost of one jail?

10. What does justice look like according to Cornel West?

CNN 10 STUDENT NEWS (**10 minute show**) *Write 5 things you learned from the news today.*

1. _____
_____
_____

2. _____
_____
_____

3. _____
_____
_____

4. _____
_____
_____

5. _____
_____
_____

Daily Goals Sheet   *****I can statements for each day.**
This is the list of things that I want to accomplish (complete) today in class.

Tasks or assignments I need to complete in class *I can exercise strategies like deep breathing (4-7-8 breathing) to calm or focus myself.	Completed? Check if "yes"
1. Entry journal prompt response & daily gratitude statement *I can recognize what I value and appreciate. *I can write a thoughtful & clear response to a writing prompt.	
2. Daily Goals Sheet filled out *I can plan short-term goals in order to reach my long term goals.	
3. CNN Student News Guided Notes 1-5 *I can summarize events in a news story.	
4. Close Reading/Literacy Activity: Today we are_____ _____ *I can complete a close reading or literacy strategy for something that I read. *I can organize and summarize information.	
Write your own goals for your school work for #s 5 and 6.	
5.	
6. *I can complete activities & lessons in my courses.	

Created by **Melissa Marini Švigelj-Smith** 2017-2019

7. Reflection sheet on goals today *I can reflect on my day and write honestly about whether or not I accomplished my short-term goals.	

In class today, my behavior goals are… Write your own personal goals for #s 3 & 4 *I can use strategies to maintain positive behaviors & reduce negative behaviors.	Did I …? Check if "yes"
1. I will keep a growth mindset.	
2. I will make healthy choices.	
3.	
4.	

"Education then, beyond all other devices of human origin,

Is a great equalizer of the conditions of men." – Horace Mann, 1848.

DAILY REFLECTION

Explain what you did well today in at least one complete sentence. _____
_____
_____

Explain how you would rate your performance in class today on a scale of 10 to 1, and explain why you ranked yourself that way. 10= I did my best 5= I tried half the time 1=I did not try at all
_____
_____
_____

Write a complete sentence about one part of your work in class you would like to improve and explain why.
_____
_____

Choose to complete at least ONE of the writing prompts below. Circle which one you are completing.
1. I wish you would have known today that I…
2. I am really proud that today I…
3. My favorite part of today was…
4. I wonder if today I could...

_____
_____
_____

Created by **Melissa Marini Švigelj-Smith** 2017-2019

First and Last Name_____ Date_____

Write one thing that you are grateful for today. **Thankful** people are happier people. Happier people are more successful people.
_____
_____

Today I am thankful for trees that clean our air!
Remember to practice 4-7-8 breathing as needed, and to keep a growth mindset.

Develop a GROWTH MINDSET - People who believe their talents can be developed (through hard work, good strategies & input from others) have a growth mindset. They tend to achieve more than those with a fixed mindset. ~Dr. Carol Dweck

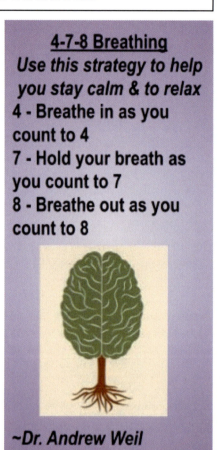

Instead of thinking...	Try thinking...
I give up	I won't stop until I succeed
I'm not good at this	How can I get better?
I can't be any better	I can always improve
This is too hard	This may take some time
I can't do this	I am going to learn to do this
My mistakes ruined me	I can learn from my mistakes
My plan didn't work	I can try another plan
I'm not smart	I can always learn new things
I'm jealous	I can learn from their success

Ismael Nazario - What I learned as a kid in jail TED Talk
Answer the questions as you watch the video. 11 minutes

1. Which state was Ismael incarcerated in?

2. What did the CO tell Ismael was "going to get him in trouble?"

3. What does Ismael suggest for youth in jail?

4. How did Ismael stay sane while he was in solitary confinement?

5. How did the "old G" help Ismael reflect on his life?

6. Name one thing that Ismael would tell his 15-year-old self.

7. Write one thing you wish you had known five years ago and explain why.

CNN STUDENT NEWS (10 minute show)
Write 5 things that you learned from the news today.

1. _____
2. _____
3. _____
4. _____
5. _____

Next, complete your **daily goals.**

Daily Goals Sheet *I can statements for each day.

This is the list of things that I want to accomplish (complete) today in class.

Tasks or assignments I need to complete in class	Completed? Check if "yes"
*I can exercise strategies like deep breathing (4-7-8 breathing) to calm or focus myself.	
1. Entry journal prompt response & daily gratitude statement *I can recognize what I value and appreciate. *I can write a thoughtful & clear response to a writing prompt.	
2. Daily Goals Sheet filled out *I can plan short-term goals in order to reach my long term goals.	
3. CNN Student News Guided Notes 1-5 *I can summarize events in a news story.	
4. Close Reading/Literacy Activity: Today we are_____ _____ *I can complete a close reading or literacy strategy for something that I read. *I can organize and summarize information.	
Write your own goals for your school work for #s 5 and 6.	
5.	
6.	

*I can complete activities & lessons in my courses.	
7. Reflection sheet on goals today *I can reflect on my day and write honestly about whether or not I accomplished my short-term goals.	

In class today, my behavior goals are… Write your own personal goals for #s 3 & 4 *I can use strategies to maintain positive behaviors & reduce negative behaviors.	Did I …? Check if "yes"
1. I will keep a growth mindset.	
2. I will make healthy choices.	
3.	
4.	

DAILY REFLECTION
Explain what you did well today in at least one complete sentence
_____
_____

Explain how you would rate your performance in class today on a scale of 10 to 1, and explain why you ranked yourself that way. 10= I did my best 5= I tried half the time 1=I did not try at all
_____
_____
_____

Write a complete sentence about one part of your work in class you would like to improve and explain why._____
_____
_____

Choose to complete at least ONE of the writing prompts below. Circle which one you are completing.
1. I wish you would have known today that I…
2. I am really proud that today I…
3. My favorite part of today was…
4. I wonder if today I could…   _____
_____
_____

M

Sebastian

Junctions Condor

8-9 Am Parental conference - Jan gen Team
9-11am Attendance Meeting

Johnny Eskews? call
Evan Kendrick - Packet request
Abigail Mateos - ? call
Ava Ingram
Arnelle Husman

Hey ye Hear Ye Hear Ye all who desire
Take paper work to Dr Wilson

end ∈ grad parade (protocol & promotional)

Alexis Crosby   912-755-2241
  Schedule 504 meeting

Alepiah's

Sarah Sego

Name_____Date_____

Write one thing that you are grateful (**thankful**) for today. Finding things to be thankful for helps improve our overall happiness. Happier people are more successful people._____
_____

Today I am thankful for passionate people.
Remember to practice 4-7-8 breathing as needed, and to keep a growth mindset.

> **Develop a GROWTH MINDSET -** *People who believe their talents can be developed (through hard work, good strategies & input from others) have a growth mindset. They tend to achieve more than those with a fixed mindset. ~Dr. Carol Dweck*

Instead of thinking...	Try thinking...
I give up	I won't stop until I succeed
I'm not good at this	How can I get better?
I can't be any better	I can always improve
This is too hard	This may take some time
I can't do this	I am going to learn to do this
My mistakes ruined me	I can learn from my mistakes
My plan didn't work	I can try another plan
I'm not smart	I can always learn new things
I'm jealous	I can learn from their success

What if We Ended the Injustice of Bail? Robin Steinberg (14 minute TED Talk)

1. What did Robin promise herself years ago?

2. Why are half-a-million Americans in jail (on any given night) even though they have not been convicted of any crime?

3. What kind of tier system has the United States' bail system created?

4. What can be an effect of being in jail for just a few days?

5. How does Robin describe a jail experience in the United States?

6. How is the American bail system also expensive?

Created by **Melissa Marini Švigelj-Smith** 2017-2019

7. What area of the American justice system in the last twenty years has created a 99% growth in jails?

8. What is the Bronx Freedom Fund?

9. What is one thing workers at the Bronx Freedom Fund learned from paying people's bail?

10. How long will bail disruptors and The Bail Project continue to fight for justice?

CNN 10 STUDENT NEWS (**10 minute show**) *Write 5 things you learned from the news today.*

1. _____
2. _____
3. _____
4. _____
5. _____

Daily Goals Sheet   *****I can statements for each day.**
This is the list of things that I want to accomplish (complete) today in class.

Tasks or assignments I need to complete in class *I can exercise strategies like deep breathing (4-7-8 breathing) to calm or focus myself.	Completed? Check if "yes"
1. Entry journal prompt response & daily gratitude statement *I can recognize what I value and appreciate. *I can write a thoughtful & clear response to a writing prompt.	
2. Daily Goals Sheet filled out *I can plan short-term goals in order to reach my long term goals.	
3. CNN Student News Guided Notes 1-5 *I can summarize events in a news story.	
4. Close Reading/Literacy Activity: Today we are_____ *I can complete a close reading or literacy strategy for something that I read. *I can organize and summarize information.	

Write your own goals for your school work for #s 5 and 6.	
5.	
6. *I can complete activities & lessons in my courses.	
7. Reflection sheet on goals today *I can reflect on my day and write honestly about whether or not I accomplished my short-term goals.	

In class today, my behavior goals are… Write your own personal goals for #s 3 & 4 *I can use strategies to maintain positive behaviors & reduce negative behaviors.	Did I …? Check if "yes"
1. I will keep a growth mindset.	
2. I will make healthy choices.	
3.	
4.	

DAILY REFLECTION

Explain what you did well today in at least one complete sentence. _____
_____

Explain how you would rate your performance in class today on a scale of 10 to 1, and explain why you ranked yourself that way. 10= I did my best 5= I tried half the time 1=I did not try at all
_____
_____

Write a complete sentence about one part of your work in class you would like to improve and explain why.
_____
_____

Choose to complete at least ONE of the writing prompts below. Circle which one you are completing.
1. I wish you would have known today that I…
2. I am really proud that today I…
3. My favorite part of today was…
4. I wonder if today I could...

_____
_____

Created by **Melissa Marini Švigelj-Smith** 2017-2019

Name_____ Date_____

Write one thing you are grateful (**thankful**) for today. Finding things to be thankful for helps improve our overall happiness. Happier people are more successful people._____
_____

Today I am thankful for things that matter.
Remember to practice 4-7-8 breathing as needed, and to keep a growth mindset.

> **Develop a *GROWTH MINDSET* -** *People who believe their talents can be developed (through hard work, good strategies & input from others) have a growth mindset. They tend to achieve more than those with a fixed mindset. ~Dr. Carol Dweck*

Instead of thinking...	Try thinking...
I give up	I won't stop until I succeed
I'm not good at this	How can I get better?
I can't be any better	I can always improve
This is too hard	This may take some time
I can't do this	I am going to learn to do this
My mistakes ruined me	I can learn from my mistakes
My plan didn't work	I can try another plan
I'm not smart	I can always learn new things
I'm jealous	I can learn from their success

4-7-8 Breathing
Use this strategy to help you stay calm & to relax
4 - Breathe in as you count to 4
7 - Hold your breath as you count to 7
8 - Breathe out as you count to 8

~Dr. Andrew Weil

What really matters at the end of life TED Talk (19 minutes)
1. How was BJ injured when he was younger?
2. What profession is BJ in now?
3. What would BJ like to bring creativity to?
4. Where does healing happen?
5. What does the role of caregivers include?
6. What is palliative care?
7. How do people at the Zen Hospice Project usher in grief when someone dies?
8. What does BJ say "can be found anywhere?"
9. What is one of the most tried and true interventions they know of at Zen Hospice?

10. What do you think BJ means when he says "Let death take us, not lack of imagination?"

_____

_____

CNN 10 STUDENT NEWS (**10 minute show**) *Write 5 things you learned from the news today.*

1. _____
   _____
   _____

2. _____
   _____
   _____

3. _____
   _____
   _____

4. _____
   _____
   _____

5. _____
   _____
   _____

Daily Goals Sheet   *I can statements for each day.
This is the list of things that I want to accomplish (complete) today in class.

Tasks or assignments I need to complete in class *I can exercise strategies like deep breathing (4-7-8 breathing) to calm or focus myself.	Completed? Check if "yes"
1. Entry journal prompt response & daily gratitude statement *I can recognize what I value and appreciate. *I can write a thoughtful & clear response to a writing prompt.	
2. Daily Goals Sheet filled out *I can plan short-term goals in order to reach my long term goals.	
3. CNN Student News Guided Notes 1-5 *I can summarize events in a news story.	
4. Close Reading/Literacy Activity: Today we are_____ _____ *I can complete a close reading or literacy strategy for something that I read. *I can organize and summarize information.	
Write your own goals for your school work for #s 5 and 6.	
5.	
6.	

*I can complete activities & lessons in my courses.	
7. Reflection sheet on goals today *I can reflect on my day and write honestly about whether or not I accomplished my short-term goals.	

In class today, my behavior goals are… Write your own personal goals for #s 3 & 4 *I can use strategies to maintain positive behaviors & reduce negative behaviors.	Did I …? Check if "yes"
1. I will keep a growth mindset.	
2. I will make healthy choices.	
3.	
4.	

"Education then, beyond all other devices of human origin,

Is a great equalizer of the conditions of men." – Horace Mann, 1848.

DAILY REFLECTION

Explain what you did well today in at least one complete sentence. _____
_____

Explain how you would rate your performance in class today on a scale of 10 to 1, and explain why you ranked yourself that way. 10= I did my best 5= I tried half the time 1=I did not try at all
_____
_____

Write a complete sentence about one part of your work in class you would like to improve and explain why.
_____
_____

Choose to complete at least ONE of the writing prompts below. Circle which one you are completing.
1. I wish you would have known today that I…
2. I am really proud that today I…
3. My favorite part of today was…
4. I wonder if today I could...

_____
_____

Created by **Melissa Marini Švigelj-Smith** 2017-2019

Name_____ Date_____

Write one thing you are grateful (**thankful**) for today. Finding things to be thankful for helps improve our overall happiness. Happier people are more successful people._____

_____

Today I'm thankful for cuddly pets!

Remember to practice 4-7-8 breathing as needed, and to keep a growth mindset.

> **Develop a GROWTH MINDSET -** *People who believe their talents can be developed (through hard work, good strategies & input from others) have a growth mindset. They tend to achieve more than those with a fixed mindset. ~Dr. Carol Dweck*

Instead of thinking...	Try thinking...
I give up	I won't stop until I succeed
I'm not good at this	How can I get better?
I can't be any better	I can always improve
This is too hard	This may take some time
I can't do this	I am going to learn to do this
My mistakes ruined me	I can learn from my mistakes
My plan didn't work	I can try another plan
I'm not smart	I can always learn new things
I'm jealous	I can learn from their success

4-7-8 Breathing
Use this strategy to help you stay calm & to relax
4 - Breathe in as you count to 4
7 - Hold your breath as you count to 7
8 - Breathe out as you count to 8

~Dr. Andrew Weil

TEDxMidwest - Writing my wrongs - Shaka Senghor
(18 minutes)

1. Who wrote the letter that changed Shaka's life?

2. Socrates says "The unexamined _____ isn't worth living."

3. What did Shaka say caused him to return to the community worse than he was when he left?

4. Why was Will ostracized in the prison by other people there?

5. What did Shaka learn from a rat?

6. What is one thing that Shaka's father taught him?

7. What did Shaka's fiancé teach him?

8. What is something Shaka learned about gun violence in our cities?

9. Shaka said when you can look at someone as a _____, you can have more empathy for them.

10. What is one of the most important things any of us can offer somebody?

<u>CNN 10 STUDENT NEWS</u> **(10 minute show)** *Write 5 things you learned from the news today.*

1. _____

2. _____

3. _____

4. _____

5. _____

Daily Goals Sheet   **I can statements for each day.*
This is the list of things that I want to accomplish (complete) today in class.

Tasks or assignments I need to complete in class *I can exercise strategies like deep breathing (4-7-8 breathing) to calm or focus myself.	Completed? Check if "yes"
1. Entry journal prompt response & daily gratitude statement *I can recognize what I value and appreciate. *I can write a thoughtful & clear response to a writing prompt.	
2. Daily Goals Sheet filled out *I can plan short-term goals in order to reach my long term goals.	
3. CNN Student News Guided Notes 1-5 *I can summarize events in a news story.	
4. Close Reading/Literacy Activity: Today we are_____ *I can complete a close reading or literacy strategy for something that I read. *I can organize and summarize information.	
Write your own goals for your school work for #s 5 and 6.	

5.	
6. *I can complete activities & lessons in my courses.	
7. Reflection sheet on goals today *I can reflect on my day and write honestly about whether or not I accomplished my short-term goals.	

In class today, my behavior goals are… Write your own personal goals for #s 3 & 4 *I can use strategies to maintain positive behaviors & reduce negative behaviors.	Did I …? Check if "yes"
1. I will keep a growth mindset.	
2. I will make healthy choices.	
3.	
4.	

DAILY REFLECTION

Explain what you did well today in at least one complete sentence.
_____
_____

Explain how you would rate your performance in class today on a scale of 10 to 1, and explain why you ranked yourself that way. 10= I did my best 5= I tried half the time 1=I did not try at all
_____
_____
_____

Write a complete sentence about one part of your work in class you would like to improve and explain why.
_____
_____
_____

Choose to complete at least ONE of the writing prompts below. Circle which one you are completing.
1. I wish you would have known today that I…
2. I am really proud that today I…
3. My favorite part of today was…
4. I wonder if today I could…

_____
_____
_____

Created by **Melissa Marini Švigelj-Smith** 2017-2019

Name_____ Date_____

Write one thing you are grateful (**thankful**) for today. Finding things to be thankful for helps improve our overall happiness. Happier people are more successful people._____
_____

Today I am thankful for smiles.

Remember to practice 4-7-8 breathing as needed, and to keep a growth mindset.

> **Develop a *GROWTH MINDSET* -** *People who believe their talents can be developed (through hard work, good strategies & input from others) have a growth mindset. They tend to achieve more than those with a fixed mindset. ~Dr. Carol Dweck*

Instead of thinking...	Try thinking...
I give up	I won't stop until I succeed
I'm not good at this	How can I get better?
I can't be any better	I can always improve
This is too hard	This may take some time
I can't do this	I am going to learn to do this
My mistakes ruined me	I can learn from my mistakes
My plan didn't work	I can try another plan
I'm not smart	I can always learn new things
I'm jealous	I can learn from their success

Answer the following questions for <u>The Science of Happiness by Soul Pancake</u>. *(8 minutes)*

1. What is the claim in the beginning about success and happiness?

2. How did experimenters put one group in a good mood for the experiment?

3. What did the control group get?

4. What were the results of the experiment?

5. What can you do to increase your own happiness and success?

Created by **Melissa Marini Švigelj-Smith** 2017-2019

CNN 10 (10 minute student news show)
*Write **5** things you learned from the news today.*

1. _____
   _____
   _____
2. _____
   _____
   _____
3. _____
   _____
   _____
4. _____
   _____
   _____
5. _____
   _____
   _____

Daily Goals Sheet   *I can statements for each day.

This is the list of things that I want to accomplish (complete) today in class.

Tasks or assignments I need to complete in class *I can exercise strategies like deep breathing (4-7-8 breathing) to calm or focus myself.	Completed? Check if "yes"
1. Entry journal prompt response & daily gratitude statement *I can recognize what I value and appreciate. *I can write a thoughtful & clear response to a writing prompt.	
2. Daily Goals Sheet filled out *I can plan short-term goals in order to reach my long term goals.	
3. CNN Student News Guided Notes 1-5 *I can summarize events in a news story.	
4. Close Reading/Literacy Activity: Today we are_____ _____ *I can complete a close reading or literacy strategy for something that I read. *I can organize and summarize information.	
Write your own goals for your school work for #s 5 and 6.	
5.	
6. *I can complete activities & lessons in my courses.	
8. Reflection sheet on goals today	

Created by **Melissa Marini Švigelj-Smith** 2017-2019

*I can reflect on my day and write honestly about whether or not I accomplished my short-term goals.	

In class today, my behavior goals are… Write your own personal goals for #s 3 & 4 *I can use strategies to maintain positive behaviors & reduce negative behaviors.	Did I …? Check if "yes"
1. I will keep a growth mindset.	
2. I will make healthy choices.	
3.	
4.	

DAILY REFLECTION

Explain what you did well today in at least one complete sentence. _____
_____

Explain how you would rate your performance in class today on a scale of 10 to 1, and explain why you ranked yourself that way. 10= I did my best 5= I tried half the time 1=I did not try at all
_____
_____

Write a complete sentence about one part of your work in class you would like to improve and explain why.
_____
_____

Choose to complete at least ONE of the writing prompts below. Circle which one you are completing.
1. I wish you would have known today that I…
2. I am really proud that today I…
3. My favorite part of today was…
4. I wonder if today I could...

_____
_____
_____

Thank you educators!
"Making a difference is always possible, especially with persistence and dedication." --Gladys De La Mora

"... if education is always to be conceived along the same antiquated lines of a mere transmission of knowledge, there is little to be hoped from it in the bettering of man's future."
Maria Montessori, The Absorbent Mind (1949)

"The way to right wrongs is to turn the light of truth upon them."
— Ida B. Wells-Barnett

"Whoever controls information, whoever controls meaning, acquires power." –Laura Esquivel

"...you know me for a tolerant man. I don't care what a man has on top of his head. All I'm interested in is what he's got inside of it."
-- Dalip Singh Saund on his 1952 campaign for judge in Westmorland

"You have to look deeper, way below the anger, the hurt, the hate, the jealousy, the self-pity, way down deeper where the dreams lie, son. Find your dream. It's the pursuit of the dream that heals you."
-- Billy Mills, recalling advice from his father
Indian name: Makata Taka Hela (respects the earth)
Tribe: Oglala Lakota (Sioux)

Made in the USA
Columbia, SC
20 January 2020